Deliver Excellent
Customer Service
With a SNAP

Deliver Excellent Customer Service With a SNAP

A No Cost Way To Restore Full Service

Philip Espinosa

WhiteBoard Design Publishing
A Coffee Cup Chat Book
snapthegap.com

Deliver Excellent Customer Service With a SNAP
© Copyright 2012 Philip Espinosa
snapthegap.com

ISBN-13: 978-1479283125
ISBN-10: 1479283126

Book design and graphics by WhiteBoard Design Graphics.
Back cover photo by Mindi Espinosa.

Additional copies of this book can be purchased from any bookstore
or ordered directly from WhiteBoard Design Publishing at the books
website: snapthegap.com.

Published by WhiteBoard Design Publishing
white-board-design.com

Printed by Createspace.com

to
Mindi

and to
all the teams that
contributed
over the past 15 years

Table of Contents

Coffee Cup Chat

Starbucks is the world's largest chain of coffee shops, with over 19,500 stores in 58 countries. You can get a cup of coffee almost anywhere. You and I both know what a coffee cup chat is. We sit and chat with others over a cup of coffee.

We meet friends, family and co-workers there. Maybe we meet new people or get introductions. Sitting in the coffee shop relaxing, chatting is an enjoyable way to spend an hour or two. What we talk about is generally not complex. Topics range from the trivial to the important to the inspirational.

I have designed databases, hired employees, held staff meetings, negotiated contracts, met new people, planned vacations, played games, listened to my kids and dreamed of the future with my wife — all at a coffee shop. Coffee cup chats.

Think of this book as a coffee cup chat. You decide if this is a trivial quick read for you. You decide if what you see here is important. You decide if you want to be inspired.

The tone used in presenting SNAP is conversational. This is not an academic treatise. There will be little in the way of charts, graphs or numbers. In fact, none. The subject matter — I believe — is critically important; however, other authors have done the studies, crunched the data and presented the colorful charts. You won't find that here.

This is a coffee cup chat book. Relax. Read it. Engage in a little give and take during the conversation shared here.

You can get through this book in an hour or two. Each section is a few pages, designed to be a quick read, and you can easily jump from place to place.

Thanks for buying this book, this cup of coffee; relax and enjoy it.

Part 1. SNAP the Customer

In this section, we cover what SNAP is and why you would want to use it. We provide a summary of the four key parts of SNAP and share with you how SNAP will help you eliminate expectation gaps.

> *It is not the employer who pays the wages. Employers only handle the money. It is the customer who pays the wages.*
> *— Henry Ford*

What Is SNAP?

SNAP is a communication technique that keeps you connected to your customer.

SNAP stands for **S**tatus, **N**ext Steps, **A**pproximate Timeline and **P**lanned Outcome.

Crafting a set of simple statements you address:
- The status of your relationship or the status of what you are doing for the customer;
- The next steps your customer should expect from you or steps you need from your customer;
- The approximate amount of time these next steps might take, or the amount of time until something else will happen;
- The planned outcome, what the customer can expect to see happen or the result of your relationship with the customer.

At the simplest level, a SNAP message is all about keeping your customer as fully informed as possible.

Using SNAP you are able to set and influence expectations, then, demonstrate how your service or product meets or exceeds those expectations.

Using SNAP you are able to establish a framework allowing you to take credit for what you already do well; and to leverage that framework to improve what you do well.

Using SNAP you anticipate your customer's concerns and deliver information before those customer concerns cause anxiety.

Reducing customer anxiety drives up customer satisfaction.

Meeting and exceeding customer expectations drives up customer satisfaction.

SNAP is an easy to use technique.

SNAP is highly effective.

SNAP is easy to learn and easy to teach.

Knowing what SNAP is and that it is easy to use, read on to see why you might want to use SNAP.

———————————

Can you benefit from using a simple communication tool to improve your customer relationships?

Do you want to know more about SNAP and how it can help you be more effective and more productive?

———————————

Why SNAP?

"Businesspeople have recognized forever that the moment when a customer interacts with a company employee is crucial to the organization's success. Traditionally, the moral that managers took from this fact was: keep your frontline employees on a tight reign; teach them to come running when they encounter anything out of the ordinary. Today... winning companies take a different tack. They understand that the frontline people themselves must be given the authority to make real-time decisions, along with the training that will help them make the right ones."

...*from What Really Works, William Joyce, Nitin Nohria and Bruce Roberson*

SNAP connects you to your customer. It gives your customer information they want and need to know. Consistent use will have a positive impact on your customer relationships.

SNAP will improve customer retention. Customer satisfaction. Help you set and guide customer expectations. SNAP will help you to be more efficient. More effective. Will reduce your stress. And, will improve your credibility.

"SNAP is a practical guide and is very useful for improving customer service and client relations. It is a must read guide for client oriented, successful managers," says Tomas Miller, Chief, Access to Finance at the Multilateral Investment Fund.

SNAP is an excellent tool that anyone can use. Right on the frontline. Right now.

Tom Roberts, Director of the Travel & Tourism Department, Pace Institute, says: "If you believe in the old sales axiom as I do, that 'the best prospects you have for new sales are customers or clients you already have,' then SNAP is an excellent training tool for sales as well as customer service."

There are two main reasons to read this book. First, you may want to improve how you deliver exceptional customer service. Second, you may want to reduce stress associated with customer relationship management.

How would you rate your overall service level today? Fair? Good? Great? Excellent?

Rate your service level.
Excellent — Great — Good — Fair — Poor

How would your customers rate your service?
Excellent — Great — Good — Fair — Poor

Consider this: What actually matters is how your customers rate your service — not how you rate it. And, your customers don't rate your "overall" service level — it doesn't matter what we want to believe, they rate each separate, individual experience. They talk about each separate experience. Unfortunately, they talk more about the negatives ones.

Check out this link. A musician sings about his flight experience. Search 'united breaks guitars.'
www.youtube.com/watch?v=5YGc4zOqozo

This is a YouTube video posted by a former United Airlines passenger who experienced less than satisfactory service. Yes, it happens. He tells his story by writing and posting a song about his experience. The lesson for us here is: this video has received over 11,000,000 views — yes, you read that correctly, over eleven million views. (Several months after starting this book, now as I complete the final review, this video has over 12 million views.) I have yet to find an absolutely positive message a customer posted about an absolutely fantastic customer experience that has received anywhere close to this amount of viewership.

So, even if you think your service standard is good enough, or if you think it is great — all it takes is one poor experience and a story told by one dissatisfied customer. No matter your current level of service, focusing on improving your service will give you a competitive advantage. Improve your service level all the time.

You might be interested in ways to improve your customer service because you have read or heard about companies, large and small, that are continually improving their customer experience — and you desire to remain competitive. For leaders and professionals at all levels in today's competitive work place, this is especially true.

If you are in business, working for yourself or a boss, you have customers. These customers are external, perhaps people that pay your company money for products or services. Or, they are internal, people in other departments of your company who rely on what you do so that the company can sell products or services.

Books, such as, "From Good to Great" by Jim Collins, "Winning" by Jack Welch, "The Toyota Way" by Jeffrey Liker or "Smart Trust" by Stephen M. R. Covey, all tell us about the value of exceptional customer service. You have probably read one of these books, or others like them. These are all exceptional books, and I highly recommend them. If you are like me, it is easy to get motivated for a short time after reading these books. Then what?

Many of us buy and read the next book to keep the "momentum" going. We want to improve. The stories in these books are motivational. We say, "Wow," reading through real world examples of executives at mega-corporations leading service turnarounds, which result in the saving of failing companies or dominance in a market sector. I have to admit, I read many of these books and they motivate me — at least for a while.

Great. However, you may be similar to me and hundreds of thousands of others: We are not all senior executives leading multi-billion dollar enterprises. I am a human resources professional supporting leaders and employees. You might be a director or manager at a hospital. Or an IT professional. Or an activities coordinator for a church. Or a pharmaceutical representative. You might be a small business owner, running an auto repair shop, or you own a hardware store, or you run your own gun shop. You might be an independent insurance broker or a financial planner.

So, what do we do? We are all busy. I don't have the luxury of delegating to teams of others. I have to deliver, busy day after busy day.

We want to provide the best customer service possible. I want to do this in the simplest way possible. Our jobs are already too busy. Some would say, way too busy to add more to the list of things we do.

What then is your bottom line?

"If you're accustomed to thinking of the bottom line only as it relates to financial matters, then you may be missing some things crucial to you and your organization. Instead, think of the bottom line as the end, the take away, the desired result."
...*from Thinking for a Change, John C. Maxwell*

SNAP neither assumes nor cares what your bottom line is. It can and will support a variety of needs and outcomes you may have.

If you own your own business, increasing your profits might motivate you.

If you earn a bonus or commission based on job performance, adding to your paycheck might motivate you.

If your job is just a j-o-b, then making your job easier might motivate you.

Increasing customer satisfaction in order to get any number of other outcomes beneficial to you may motivate you.

If any of this resonates with you, continue reading to learn more about SNAP.

Are you motivated to improve your business?

Do you realistically know how your customers rate your service?

Do you see one or more ways that SNAP can benefit you?

Do you have one or more specific things you would like to improve about your relationship with key customers?

———————————

Two Analogies

SNAP is, quite literally, a snap. This means it is simple. Please understand that simple does not mean easy or trivial.

SNAP is not a diagnostic, data collection or analysis methodology. It is a simple way of thinking and communicating with customers that can be incorporated into any step of any workflow or interaction with your customers. It does not take hours of training before you can use it.

Let me use two analogies to help explain SNAP.

For our first analogy, let's consider a master carpenter. Norm, from the well-known PBS series comes to mind. He has a workshop. He is skilled, and he has cool tools. Of course, he completes impressive projects because he knows what he is doing, and he also uses all those tools to make the work he does easier, more consistent, to add a cleaner finish, to add needed detail. Norm has his professional skills, built up over the course of his career, and he has excellent tools in his tool kit.

Snap is one of your tools. Think of yourself as a master craftsman for whatever line of work you are in. SNAP doesn't care what you do. You care, and that is why you need to make sure you have more than a few cool tools in your tool kit. You have significant professional skill, built up over the course of your career, and you have excellent tools in your tool kit. SNAP wants to be one those tools.

For both you and Norm, the tools don't make you a master, it is your knowledge of the tools, how to use them consistently, how to connect the tools to what your work demands.

Using specialized tools and techniques will make your work easier, giving you consistent, reliable results. SNAP will deliver consistent, reliable results. Put it in your toolbox. Make it one of your go to tools. The more you use it, the more you will want to use it because of the value you get from using the tool. **SNAP adds polish to your work.**

For our second analogy, let's consider a photographer. We know how the photographer works with her camera so we will only consider the basic aspects of what is involved (apologies to professional photographers).

Using a camera the photographer takes pictures and can easily share those pictures with others. The photographer's experience can be very private and personal. The image the photographer sees, while adjusting the focus and framing the shot, is seen by the photographer and no one else. It is only after the photographer takes the picture that there is anything to share.

The photographer's finger moves, we hear the mechanical click (or the digital simulation on our digital camera or phone) and the result is what we call a snap shot. The snap completes the picture. We have all experienced friends saying, "Let me see" after we took a picture, so we turn our digital camera around and show off the picture we just took.

With today's digital cameras and large viewing screens, a group of people may see the image being framed. The group experiences the snap when the image is captured, and the picture is then instantly emailed off to others or shared on a service like Facebook.

For this analogy to help us, we are focused on what happens when the picture is taken. That picture, whether shared with those nearby or posted on-line, represents a shared experience. There is enough information in that picture for those of us who see it to have a shared experience.

Think of the proud mother who takes a picture of her daughter blowing out candles on a birthday cake. The picture is emailed to Grandma. Minutes later on the phone, the mother and grandmother laugh and cry and talk about the cake, the kid's smile and the colored balloons. Clearly, the snap completed the picture and gave both the mother and the grandmother a shared understanding of the birthday party.

SNAP is one tool in the master carpenter's toolbox — use it in your quest to improve customer service. It can be an extremely important tool.

Like the moment of taking a picture, **SNAP completes the picture**. This allows us all to understand and share a common experience.

SNAP removes ambiguity. Provides information and predictability. Sets expectations.

SNAP is deceptively simple. It can be used by anyone. With consistent use, it can be mastered. You won't master it overnight. In fact, first time users may struggle to master SNAP because it appears so simple they will think little or no investment is needed to use it.

While it is true that SNAP can be used "out of the box" — plug and play — careful, purposeful use will, over time, give you consistently better results.

Does your toolkit have room for one more specialized tool?

Can you see yourself using a simple, and extremely effective tool, like SNAP, in conjunction with other effective strategies?

Have You Ever Wondered?

Have you ever wondered —

- Why your customers call with simple questions
- Why you hear the same questions from your customers over and over
- How you can reduce customer complaints
- How you can improve customer satisfaction
- How you can reduce misunderstandings around what service or product you deliver to your customers
- How you can improve your relationship with your customers
- How you can give your customers a better understanding of where they stand in your time line
- How you can remove customer interruptions from your daily routine
- How you can free up time in your busy day
- How you can be more productive
- How you can improve your repeat customer count
- How you can reduce your customer's stress and uncertainty levels
- How you can reduce your stress levels

- How you can increase the consistency of your customer interactions
- How you can be more efficient in your customer communications
- What if I could do something about all the items listed above

SNAP is a simple tool set that will do just that — it will help you address all of the items noted above — and many more.

SNAP, when used consistently, will:
- Improve customer satisfaction
- Increase your productivity
- Improve your sales
- Return precious time to your busy day
- Reduce your stress
- Improve your credibility with your customer and your team

There is no reason not to use SNAP.

Is being more effective and less stressful important to you?

Do you see benefits in both significantly improving your professional credibility and your customer satisfaction at the same time?

The Four Parts of SNAP

Scott James, software engineer and university professor says: "Developing quality software systems is a complex problem. Too many times customers are involved heavily in the development process up front during requirements engineering and analysis, then feel abandoned later on as design and implementation occur. SNAP is a critical tool to keep customers aware of what's taking place the entire time the system is being developed. As this book notes, it is so easy to integrate SNAP into any existing workflow, so no company, team or individual has any reason to not reach new levels of customer service satisfaction."

SNAP is not a process you follow, rather it is a tool that can be used in any of your workflows. It is specifically designed to help your customers feel confident in their relationship with you. It helps you manage your time by being proactive, anticipating your customer's needs and addressing those needs before the customer is even aware of them.

SNAP complements existing workflows. More details on this in the section titled How SNAP Works.

No matter how much reading you do, you will only master SNAP by using it. So, use it out of the box. Then, invest in SNAP and master it. This user guide will get you started and will help you master SNAP.

The parts of SNAP are:

1. Status

2. Next steps

3. Approximate timeline

4. Planned outcome

The four parts of SNAP can also be thought of as questions. Answer these questions for your customers. Do this before they ask the question.

What is the status of ___?

What are the next steps for ___?

What is the approximate time line for ___?

What is the planned outcome of ___?

Our customers perceive they are getting less than acceptable service when they have unanswered questions.

When used properly, in a proactive way, SNAP answers the questions up front. Take SNAP to the next level and answer these same questions at a later touch point with the customer.

Putting multiple SNAPs into various segments of existing workflows easily does this.

Our goal is to provide information to the customer in a reliable and predictable way. By doing this, we reduce and then eliminate any gap in the customer's perception about the service we deliver. In fact, when mastered, we significantly improve the customer's perception of our service levels.

In a world where perception is reality, SNAP is extremely powerful.

Knowing where expectations don't match allows us to see where we can use the power of SNAP to close the expectation Gap.

———————————

Do you see benefits in creating greater alignment between the expectations shared by you and your customer?

Do you have the personal ability to use the four parts of SNAP to significantly reduce the expectation gap?

———————————

The Gap

What is the Gap?

"Exactly what are we confronting? We are stepping up to a: broken promise — a gap; a difference between what you expected and what actually happened."
...from Crucial Confrontations, Kerry Patterson, Joseph Grenny, Ron McMillan and Al Switzler

Worded for our purposes, we can say the Gap is the difference between what your customer expected and what they actually experienced. The Gap occurs when you and your customer have a different understanding of your business relationship or the nature of a particular transaction. The Gap is a lack of alignment with the customer. Use SNAP to set expectations when you begin a customer experience. Our goal is to eliminate the Gap. We want perfect alignment.

For our purposes in this user guide, anyone you do business with or for is your customer.

Tom Roberts worked for over 18 years in the travel industry. Dynamic. Fast paced. Where the dreams and expectations of customers are high. Alignment and managing the Gap was vital to his success. Tom says: "Communication is the key to properly implement SNAP. As I found out from personal experience, this is especially true when confronted by an irate client. I see a real need for an approach like SNAP."

Here are common Gaps, which you may be aware of or experienced:

Ordering a steak well done and getting it rare.

Calling an 800-customer service number and being placed on hold.

Coming home from a long day at work and finding your cable signal is out.

Making a call to a company and getting a multilayered phone tree.

Sitting in the doctor's office waiting room, and waiting.

Leaving your car at the shop for routine work and finding it is not ready when you return to pick it up.

Sending a resume in for a new job and not knowing when you might get a response.

Volunteering to help at your local church and not getting a call back.

Coming to work only to find the user interface on your favorite program looks different.

When working with a financing agent, getting high expectations regarding potential funding for your project and then not knowing where you are in the approval process.

Applying for a license to operate a business and not receiving the permit within the expected time frame without an explanation regarding the delay.

Sitting in the ER and not knowing if your wait will be measured in minutes or hours.

Add in some Gaps from your personal perspective:

1.

2.

3.

All these experiences, and many others similar to them, have something in common. There is a Gap in what the customer experiences or thinks is going on compared to what the service provider thinks.

All too often, the expectation Gap is driven by two things: 1) waiting, and, 2) outcome differences.

The Gap occurs when any two people engage in an exchange. The way we routinely communicate results in a Gap. The Gap happens when I make a request and you give me an answer, but the answer does not fully tell me what I think I need to know.

What do customers want to know? Customers want to know about the status, the next steps, the approximate amount of time it will take for things to happen, and what the planned outcome is going to be. In short, customers want to know SNAP.

Let us look at an example in a little more detail.

Ordering a burger and waiting too long. You go into your favorite fast food restaurant for lunch (let's call it Favorites) and order a burger. You normally expect to wait about two minutes. Your wait is now five minutes. You look at your watch; it is now noon. How much longer? You start doing some self-talk, telling yourself things that are not complimentary about the restaurant or service you are getting. Really, you are not sure why you are here today. You start counting the number of employees working behind the counter; wow, sure are a lot of people working back there. You just know something is going on and it is not good. You hope this does not affect your lunch. Why now? Why today? Why you? After all, you are in a hurry.

From another perspective, this story might look different. Let's say you work at Favorites; it is a good job and helps you pay the bills. The normal lunch crowd is arriving. You have been telling the customers that the wait is the usual two minutes, and you look at the timer on the register, noting the wait is a little longer. The manager circles through the back area quickly stopping by each employee. "We have a big order coming in," he says. "A tour bus with a big country star is pulling through. We've been asked not to tell the name; they don't want to be mobbed. Should be on the news tonight. Let's get this order processed now." How exciting. Checking your watch, you note it is almost noon, about five minutes before the hour. Excited, you start processing the larger order for the tour bus.

What is going on here? The Favorites employee does not think he is giving poor service. In fact, he is working harder than usual due to the large order that just came in. He thinks he is delivering great service and is stepping up to handle this challenge.

The customer is still waiting. He perceives he is getting poor service; all he knows is that he is still waiting. It may only be five or six minutes now, however, if the normal wait is two minutes, then a six-minute wait is 3x longer than normal. Comparatively, speaking, that is a long wait. Any minute now, the customer is going to step up to the counter and complain and ask about the order. The moment this happens, we have an upset customer. In fact, we have an upset customer whether he asks what is going on or if he just keeps on waiting.

What are our options? Consider this: The employee who is taking orders and managing the front counter quietly goes over to the waiting customer and says: "Excuse me sir, I know you just placed your order, however, right after we put your order through we also got slammed with a very large order from a tour bus — some really famous country star, they won't tell us who it is, but, I think it will be on the news tonight. Anyway, your sandwich is being made right now and will take a few minutes longer. Usual wait time for us about two to three minutes, we should be able to get your meal out in a little over five minutes. I hope that is not too much of an inconvenience. Will that be ok?"

The customer just got SNAPed; he heard the status of his order, he heard about next steps, he heard the approximate timeline and he heard the planned outcome. The customer says: "Sure, that will be fine. Who is on the bus?"

"I am sorry sir, I really don't know, the only thing they told us was that it might be on the news; and we got a really big order. Hey, this is exciting, I gotta get back to processing it — your meal will be up in a few more minutes. Really appreciate your patience. If anything changes, I will let you know immediately."

Yup. SNAPed.

Better yet, he heard the promise of a follow-up SNAP if things were to change. Mastery.

The employee at the counter shared a quick overview of **status**, told the customer what the **next steps** were, mentioned an **approximate timeline** and committed to a specific **planned outcome**. And, to seal the SNAP deal, the employee provided assurances that a SNAP follow-up would take place.

What actually happens with the customer is the same, whether SNAP occurs or not. This customer is going to wait a little over six minutes for his meal. If, after two minutes, the customer is not briefed, Favorites will end up with an unhappy customer — and it matters not one bit how much harder or faster the employees are working. The customer only cares about his order.

Once SNAPed, the customer has a great understanding about what to expect, he no longer speculates, imaging all kinds of horrible or disastrous things about his order, the restaurant's incompetence, or _____ (fill in the blank). The trouble with letting the uninformed customer fill in the blank is that the story about lunch will be the customer's negative story, and will be told to many people. The story will not help Favorites' reputation.

Once SNAPed, the customer knows what is going on and, in fact, in our case, has a new, exciting replacement story. Tonight, watching the news, he will say: "I was there!"

Gaps are opportunities. Look for them, for you will surely see and experience them almost everywhere.

Do you see the danger in the Gap and how it affects your customer experiences?

Have you given thought to the Gap you have with your customers?

To you actively look for or listen for the Gap?

Can you image working with customers and not having to deal with broken promises?

Really, Is That All?

Deceptively simple; yet, hard to do.

Think back to the story about the fast food restaurant and the customer's lunch order. It is so easy to respond to this story by saying, "Really, is that all?"

At the simplest level, the answer is: "Yes, that's it. That's what SNAP is all about. That is all."

It can be that easy.

Toni R. Linn, independent consultant, says: "SNAP provides the principles that guide me when working on any of the issues I encounter supporting my clients — such as updating an employee's insurance coverage to writing proposals for submission to a Board of Directors. SNAP allows me to keep everyone with a need to know updated and informed."

Here's a challenge: Take one day — perhaps a Saturday — as you shop, do your chores, or go out for a meal pay close attention to the customer service you get. Go beyond just thinking if those helping you are friendly or likable. Listen for something that sounds or feels like SNAP.

When you get what you feel is great service, break it down. Was the service truly great because of something sophisticated or complex? Or, was it great because of something simple? Did you get attention? Did you get information? Was it real time? Was it similar to SNAP?

I bet nine out of ten times it was great service because of something as simple as SNAP. Studies show that excellent service brings you back as a return customer, and that this is a stronger pull than the quality of the product. For example, memorable dining experiences always center on outstanding service.

If you experience service that was less than great — do the same thing: break it down. Was the service less than great because of something that was absolutely horrible? Or, was it less than great because of a simple lack of attention, insufficient information, or you felt like you waited longer than you needed to? Perhaps something as simple as SNAP was missing.

I will bet nine out of ten times the less than great experience could have been great only if — something as simple as SNAP took place. Studies show that an excellent product is not enough to bring customers back. You can always go find an excellent product somewhere else, along with excellent service. Never underestimate the absolute need for outstanding customer service.

So, yes, at the most basic level, that is all there is to it.

SNAP is simple; it is not complex.

However, just because it is simple does not mean it is easy. You have to make an effort for SNAP to be effortless.

Let's take a closer look at how SNAP works.

Are you willing to invest some personal and professional time to work past the simplicity of SNAP?

Can you imagine yourself being on the receiving end of a simple SNAP message, and feeling better about the service you expect to get?

How SNAP Works

Paul Graham, author and programmer is quoted as saying: "For [a product] to surprise me, it must be satisfying expectations I didn't know I had."

Use SNAP to set and steer these expectations. This is what you want from SNAP. To set expectations and to meet and exceed those expectations. It is good to surprise your customer by exceeding expectations. It is not good to surprise your customer by failing their expectations.

The four parts of SNAP all work together and are best used when snapped into your key workflows.

We all have workflows. Some formal, some less formal. Any pattern of work that you use on a regular basis is a workflow. At times we document these and call them Standard Operating Procedures or SOPs. You might call them policies or processes. Whatever called, the patterns of what you do are your workflows.

Does SNAP care about your workflow? No, not really. Will SNAP require you to change your workflow? Again, no, not really.

The not really part of the above answers is that SNAP is not a workflow analysis process and is not used to improve workflows. Purposeful use of SNAP may result in you seeing your workflows differently. As you use SNAP, you will return to the structure of your key workflows, and, most likely, you will edit, update and improve your workflows. However, as you get started with SNAP, use existing workflows. Basically, SNAP will easily snap into any part of your current workflows.

We will not be spending time on building or deconstructing workflows in this book; there are many other resources for that. We will reference how SNAP fits into existing workflows, since that is an important way to harness the power of SNAP. However, this coffee cup chat will focus on how to put a SNAP message together and how to leverage SNAP.

Let's look at a high level, generic customer workflow. Trigger > Processing > Completion.

Adding a little more detail, yet still staying high level, your workflows may share some of these steps:

1.   Greeting
2.   Request / Order / Trigger
3.   Acknowledgement / Acceptance
4.   Processing / Work Steps / Tasks
5.   Check In / Status Update
6.   Completion

SNAP will fit easily into any step of your current workflow. We will go into the details of setting up a good SNAP a little later, so for now let's continue to look at this from a high level.

Pick one of your most routinely used or triggered workflows. To get started, I suggest you snap a SNAP into your workflow right at the start of the engagement.

- Greeting
- Request / Order / Trigger
- SNAP

Here's an example from work I do. As a human resource leader, I spend a lot of time hiring people. This is one of my most routine workflows. This process is triggered by a request from a manager. The first few steps of this process are: Request To Hire A New Employee Submitted > Request Approved > Job Posted.

The request process is routine. It all happens by email or other electronic process. It happens by phone and it happens in person-to-person conversation. It happens several times a day. And, just as routinely, I would get questions from managers asking: "Did my request get received?" "Did the request get approved?" "Did the job get posted?"

The workflow does not necessarily need to be edited or changed for me to improve customer service. All I have to do is add in one or more SNAPs. In Section 2 we will walk through writing sample SNAP statements.

This is what we did to the job request process. Request Submitted > SNAP > Request Approved > SNAP > Job Posted > SNAP > SNAP ...

SNAP is a positive, informative message that you purposefully insert into key places in your key workflows. The repeating of these messages both informs your customers and frames their perception of the relationship they have with you.

When you don't give your customers the information provided by a SNAP, your customers will fill in the blank spots on their own. They will guess at the information they don't get from you. Don't leave your customers guessing; use SNAP to guide and steer perception and to deliver improved customer service.

SNAP messages will fit into almost any part of your workflow. Consider the generic example from earlier in this section; add in SNAPS.

1. Greeting > SNAP

2. Request / Order / Trigger > SNAP

3. Acknowledgement / Acceptance > SNAP

4. Processing / Work Steps / Tasks > SNAP

5. Check In / Status Update > SNAP

6. Completion > SNAP

Perception does not change overnight, however, considering the example shared above about posting jobs, after a few months the overall perception was that requests to fill jobs and the posting of jobs took place in half the time it had taken previously. The only real change was the addition of SNAPs. Managers were much happier. The HR team was able to spend less time responding to questions about the status of things, and to move the communications of the relationship to more productive topics.

SNAP works as part of key workflows. It also works at another, more basic level. Here is an example: "When a computer chimes or a smartphone vibrates with a new message, the brain starts anticipating the momentary distraction that opening an email provides. That expectation, if unsatisfied, can build until a meeting is filled with antsy [people] checking their buzzing Blackberrys under the table." So writes Charles Duhigg in The Power of Habit. Duhigg helps us understand there are three major phases to a habit: a cue, a routine and a reward. Much of this takes place in our sub-conscience.

Why is this important to SNAP? Using SNAP consistently lets you establish the cue, the routine and the reward for your customer. Your workflow is the core part of the routine. The expectations you have set, or are influencing, form the basis for the reward. SNAP connects your customer to the cue, that which starts or initiates your relationship. SNAP connects your customer to the routine, your process, by informing them of the status and next steps. And, SNAP connects your customer to the reward, the planned outcome. As you dig into SNAP, understand it is simple, yet sophisticated — all at the same time.

Cue > Routine > Reward

Status > Next Steps/Approximate Time > Planned Outcome

Because of this simplicity, because of this connection with our habits, SNAP is extremely powerful. And, the good news is, it can be used immediately. You don't need to over analyze the science behind it. Look for an opportunity to get your message to your customer.

The importance of workflows is that they provide a routine delivery vehicle for us. All of our key or core customer transactions are driven by workflows. A customer comes into your restaurant (the cue); you have a workflow to greet and connect the customer with a table (the routine); the customer expects to get seated so dinner can be ordered (the reward). A customer drives into your auto repair shop (the cue); you have a workflow to welcome your customer and connect them to services you provide (the routine). The customer expects to get their car repaired (the reward).

We have all been in one or more situations like these. Our behavior in these circumstances is driven by habit. Understand that you have workflows. These workflows are culturally connected to your customer's habits — your habits as well. You can influence outcomes by using SNAP.

In one or more places of your key workflows, just insert one or more SNAPs.

"People tend to look at their business from the inside out—that is, they get so focused on making and selling their products that they lose awareness of the needs...of their customers."
...from Execution, The Discipline of Getting Things Done, Larry Blossidy and Ram Charan

Using SNAP messages forces you to look at what you are doing from the viewpoint of the customer.

Make SNAP work for you. Add it into key locations of your key workflows. Workflows are awesome delivery vehicles for SNAP.

Invest some time and thought, then pull the trigger: plug and play. Won't cost you a dime.

Do you have workflows that you follow during the course of a routine day?

Do some of your workflows intersect with your customers?

Can you see how powerful SNAP can be when dropped into your routine customer focused workflows?

No Cost, Really?

The title of this book proclaims "A No Cost Way to Restore Full Service". Really? No cost? Here's the simple answer: Yes, really, no cost.

Of course, nothing is really no cost. It cost you a little bit to get this book, and it cost you some time to read it. And it may cost you some time to share SNAP with your team. And it may cost you some time to experiment with different versions of a SNAP statement to find the one that work best for you. You may also have a modest investment if you fly me in to conduct training for your organization.

However, you will not need to invest a lot of money, you will not need to plan a budget in order to afford SNAP, you will not need a chief financial officer to do a return on investment analysis. You will not need your computer systems department to approve complex technology. You don't need to set up a savings plan and save up for months or years. You don't need to swap out expensive equipment in order to afford SNAP.

I could go on and on. But, I think you get the idea. You can get SNAP up and running right here and right now. It is truly plug and play.

"One of our challenges involves communication — between office staff, doctor and staff, or staff and patient," says Whitney Kuhne, a dental assistant with over thirteen years of direct patient care experience. She goes on to say, "Working in a dental office is stressful enough! If we are not constantly communicating it leads to future problems and more unneeded stress. And the only people who suffer are the patients. SNAP is an excellent and easy way to communicate with everyone in the office, and it costs nothing. This lets you concentrate on what matters the most to you...your patients. Thanks SNAP!"

SNAP is no cost. It is yours. Run with it!

So, yes, the cover of the book accurately proclaims SNAP is a no cost way to restore full service. Now, let's look at how to put the four no cost parts of SNAP together.

Are you willing to invest in "no cost" approach?

Are improved customer relationships, improved business outcomes and improved personal effectiveness important to you?

What would the impact of improved customer service be to your company?

What would the impact of improved customer service be to you professionally?

Are you willing to invest personal and professional time in learning about, experimenting with and mastering SNAP?

_____

Part 2. Put It All Together

In this section, we cover the four key parts of SNAP in more detail, provide examples for each part of SNAP and then help you put them all together. We present samples and then compile those samples into complete SNAP statements.

> *Quality in a service or product is not what you put into it. It is what the client or customer gets out of it.*
> — *Peter Drucker*

The Parts of SNAP

Let's look briefly at the various parts that make up SNAP. We will then look at each part in more detail, sharing a bit more insight into how you can best use and leverage SNAP.

SNAP stands for —

- **S**tatus
- **N**ext Steps
- **A**pproximate Timeline
- **P**lanned Outcome

A SNAP statement is made up of four parts. A great SNAP statement is approximately two to five simple sentences — put together they deliver the SNAP message. Don't measure your SNAP statement quality by how many sentences are in it — two to five sentences is just a guide. If you write statements that are longer, look at them to make sure that, for your needs, longer is better. I find that shorter, to the point, is better. That way you can deliver a SNAP message in 30 seconds.

Let's look at the four parts of SNAP.

Status. Mention the status of: A request; an order; current wait times.

Next Steps. Mention what specific next steps the customer can expect. Mention more than just the immediate next step; mention two or three steps that follow.

Approximate Timeline. Mention how long the current status will exist, how long it will be until the next step is completed, and the due date for the planned outcome. This timeline might be in minutes if you are selling burgers, and might be days or weeks if you are doing custom work or building software solutions.

Planned Outcome. Mention what the customer can expect to see, get, receive, and have delivered. It doesn't matter if they know what they ordered or requested, tell them anyway. And, many times, we have customers, especially internal customers, who may submit requests and not really know what they are going to get. Tell them.

Here, a word of advice: keep the tone of your SNAP message conversational; keep it consistent with your customer experience. You know what is best here. I find that conversational, informal, everyday language works best.

Let's revisit the fast food lunch order from earlier in the book.

"Excuse me, sir, I know you just placed your order, however, right after we put your order through we also got slammed with a very large order from a tour bus — some really famous country star, they won't tell us who it is, but, I think it will be on the news tonight. Anyway, your sandwich is being made right now and will take a few minutes longer. Usual wait time for us about two to three minutes, we should be able to get your meal out in a little over five minutes. I hope that is not too much of an inconvenience. Will that be ok?"

This statement is five sentences, including the closing question. I admit, the first sentence does run on, however, it fits the tone and circumstance for the customer. The tone is conversational and comforting.

Here is some other advice — what not to do. I have experienced some SNAP users walking through a SNAP message just like they were reading a script. You have heard that, too, at times when placing a to-go order at a restaurant.

"I would like a burger, fries and soda to go."

"Will that be for here or to go?"

There you go, that is a script. Autopilot. You don't want your SNAPs to be autopilots. Here's another approach to avoid.

"Ok, so I need to tell you about the status of _____. Now let me tell you what the next steps are; they are _____. Now I will let you know what the approximate time line is; it will be ____ for us to follow-up. The planned outcome at the end of all this is _____."

Don't laugh. After reading this example, you might be saying to yourself that you would never deliver a SNAP message like this. However, the example above is drawn from my personal experiences in coaching others about SNAP; I can't make this stuff up.

This is a good SNAP message:

"Your request to post a full time analyst has been approved today and was posted today. Jobs are posted for five days, after which we will refer the top 10 qualified candidates to you. Your recruiter for this job is Bob."

Three sentences.

Here's another way I have seen less than perfect statements. We do use email a lot, and the above message will easily go into an email. See the sample and please don't do this: "Status: analyst posted. Next steps: candidates will apply; will send over to you. Approx time: will send applicants after job closes. Planned outcome: you fill the job."

Once again, this is taken from real life. Please don't do this. You may be able to check off a box and say to your boss or team, "Yeah, I used a SNAP message," but this type of message does not help you.

As you put the parts of SNAP together, don't settle. Push yourself to write and use purposeful, conversational and meaningful messages.

You will notice in the example of good SNAP statements that the words status, next steps, approximate timeline and planned outcome are rarely used. We can tell these things to our customer without being blatant about it.

Like Norm, the master carpenter, who uses specialized tools to do polished and professional work, use SNAP to add polish and a high level of professionalism to your customer interactions.

A quick start approach to SNAP is to draft out ideas for each of the four parts of SNAP. Then, just put them together. To ensure a highly effective message, as you draft and compile the four parts of SNAP, remember this axiom: less is more.

These four parts of SNAP all work together. One does not work well without the others. Let's look at each part in greater detail.

Do you see how easily the four parts of SNAP work with each other?

Do you have time during the course of a routine day,
dealing with routine customer issues, to draft out and
use three sentences to improve outcomes?

If you had to choose, using SNAP or dealing with
regular customer issues, which would you choose?

Is it worth your effort to add another specialized tool to
your toolkit?

———————————————

Status

Let's look at Status in more detail, the first part of SNAP.

This is where you specifically mention the status of where things are right now, today. This might be the status of an order that has been placed. The status of wait times. The status of progress or findings.

Here are some examples. Reviewing these examples is the best way to get a good feel for status. Note two things: 1) The sample statements do not rely on the word status; 2) These samples are brief and are not presented within any context — when combined with other parts of SNAP and placed within a real life situation or context you will customize and them for the realities of your situations.

The status of a request to fill a vacant position: Your request has been received and is approved.

The status of wait times at a restaurant: Welcome and thank you for choosing us for dinner this evening; we do have a short wait for a table.

The status of your car repair: Your car is next in line; we are ahead of schedule today.

The status of a multistage project: We have completed stages 1 and 2 and are starting stage 3.

The status of a back order product: Your order has been successfully submitted and is currently on back order.

The status of adding a new dependent to insurance coverage: All your documents are complete, and have been successfully submitted to the insurance company.

There are many more examples that can be used; the wording in these examples can easily be modified to best fit your needs. And, new or other examples can be drafted for your specific use.

When you are a customer, is knowing the status of something important to you?

Do you think knowing the status is important to your customers?

Can you find time to let your customers know the status that is important to them?

———————————————

Next Steps

Let's look at Next Steps in more detail, the second part of SNAP.

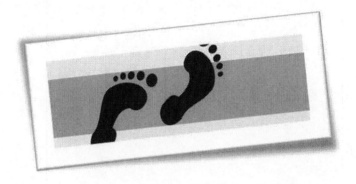

This is where you specifically mention or list the next steps that will take place or need to take place. Make a point of mentioning more than the next immediate step; mention two or three important steps, things with which the customer can connect. This is not your opportunity to educate the customer about the finer points of your workflow. It is the time to let your customer know that you will be doing important things for them and what those important things are.

The next steps to fill a vacant position: Your request will be posted and we will send you the top 10 qualified applicants.

The next steps as you wait for a seat at a restaurant: Here is a pager; we will buzz you when your table is ready; in the meantime, please make yourself comfortable in our lounge.

The next steps as your car is being repaired: We will run a diagnostic, let you know what we find and with your approval complete the repairs.

The next steps of a multistage project: The work team will meet twice within the next week to discuss their findings for outlining stage 3.

The next steps of a back order product: You will be notified via email when your order is filled; the email will include the shipping date and expected date of delivery; we will call to follow-up and make sure everything is all right with your purchase.

The next steps of adding a new dependent to insurance coverage: The insurance company will review and process your request; you will receive a new health insurance card once your dependent has been added.

There are many more examples that can be used; the wording in these examples can easily be modified to best fit your needs. And, new or other examples can be drafted for your specific use.

When you are a customer, is knowing what the next steps are important to you?

Do you think it is important for your customer to know what the next steps are?

Can you find time to let your customers know what the next steps are?

Approximate Timeline

Let's look at Approximate Timeline in more detail, the third part of SNAP.

This is where you specifically describe how long the next steps will take or how long the wait is until the planned outcome, or even, how long it will be before you deliver another SNAP, updating the customer. This is not the time to explain how long your workflow takes, or about all the hard work you are going to put into the workflow. This is the time for you to give a realistic preview to the customer about timing. Timing might be in minutes, hours, days or months. For most real time SNAPs, timing will be measured in minutes, hours or days.

Timing messages also include communicating the timing for follow-up SNAPs. This is especially true when your workflow is designed to find or discover things during the course of the customer relationship.

The approximate timeline to fill a vacant position: The job will be posted for five days and we will send you qualified applicants in the three days that follow closing the posting.

The approximate timeline for you to wait for a seat at the restaurant: The wait for a table in the front room is about 45 minutes and for a table in the patio the wait is less than 30 minutes.

The approximate timeline for your car to be repaired: It will take two hours to run some tests; we will give you a call in two hours and let you know what we find.

This type of service provider is well served by linking SNAP messages. Time is spent to assess what other services are needed. SNAP follow-ups are critical.

The approximate timeline of a multistage project: A draft of stage 3 will be completed two weeks from today.

The approximate timeline of a back order product: Due to this product being on back order we do not have a fulfillment date; we will contact you in 10 days to give you an update regarding the back order status. Do you want to continue with your order for this product?

The approximate timeline of adding a new dependent to insurance coverage: It takes the insurance company about two weeks to do the initial processing; you can expect your dependent to show on your coverage within the next 30 days. The effective date is the beginning of next month.

There are many more examples that can be used; the wording in these examples can easily be modified to best fit your needs. And, new or other examples can be drafted for your specific use.

When you are a customer, is knowing the approximate timeline important to you?

Do you think it is important for your customers to know what the approximate timeline is?

Can you find time to let your customers know what the timeline is?

Planned Outcome

Let's look at Planned Outcome in more detail, the fourth and final part of SNAP.

This is where you specifically state what the planned outcome of the transaction or business relationship will be. Again, this is not where you tell the customer how hard you are working. It is where you help keep the customer focused on what you will deliver. You want the customer to connect with the purpose of their relationship with you. This is all about the planned or desired outcome. What will be done. What will be delivered. What they will get.

The planned outcome to fill a vacant position: You will receive the top 10 qualified candidates.

The planned outcome for you to wait for a seat at the restaurant: We will have your table ready.

The planned outcome for your car to be repaired: After we run some tests, we will tell you what repairs your car needs.

The planned outcome of a multistage project: With the completion of stage 3, the project will be completed and ready for submission to the Board for final approval.

The planned outcome of a back order product: We will let you know when your product is available for shipment; we want you to enjoy this gadget with your new laptop.

The planned outcome of adding a new dependent to insurance coverage: Your dependent will then be covered under your insurance plan and will be able to present his/her insurance card for treatment.

There are many more examples that can be used; the wording in these examples can easily be modified to best fit your needs. And, new or other examples can be drafted for your specific use.

This is the last of the four sections. All you need to do is combine the four parts of SNAP and then share your SNAP messages with your customers.

———————————

When you are a customer, do you want to know what the planned outcome is?

Is it important for your customers to know what the planned outcome is?

Can you find time to let your customers know what the planned timeline is?

Can you see how these parts of SNAP help to drive customer expectations?

———————————

Complete SNAPs

Tom Roberts says of his career in the corporate travel industry, "Our corporate travel consultants practiced the SNAP concept; we just did not have a name for it. This program brings it all into focus!"

To write an effective SNAP statement, make notes about each of the four parts of SNAP. We saw this in the examples shared in the previous four sections. Then take these notes and put them together in a final, complete statement. Edit more, as needed.

When drafting SNAP statements, keep two key things in mind:

First, use caution with your choice of words. Pay particular attention when using the words they or someone. Check your SNAP for these words. While use of the words they or someone may be okay at times, these words can be very dangerous. If these words do not directly refer to someone (or something) you already referenced alarms should be going off in your head. The person or items these words refer to must be real, must have real names, you should know exactly who or what they are.

Do not use they or someone to avoid taking ownership or responsibility. Example: "I am sorry we are behind schedule. They told me to call and let you know. Someone will get with you later." Compare this to: "I am sorry we are behind schedule. Bob, our product manager, asked that I contact you in person. Bob is working with other members of the team and we expect the back order to be cleared by the end of the week. Either Bob or I will get with you no later than Thursday to confirm shipment. Is there anything else I can do for you right now?"

Second, avoid using negative words; don't talk anyone or anything down — not anyone on your team, not anyone on the competitor's team, not your product, not your service, not your process. Always speak positively. Use the word yes when answering questions. Ask questions that elicit a yes response. Using positive language sets a positive expectation for your customer.

The best way to see this in action is to look at each of those examples as a full SNAP message.

For each example below, we show the four separate parts, and then we show a completed SNAP statement. While the words used in the completed statements might be very similar to the draft words used in each of the four separate parts, the completed statements are edited or rewritten to best suit the situation. Each completed statement could be rewritten in any number of ways. Your choices, when it comes to writing your final SNAP statements, depend largely on the context, circumstance and tone that are most appropriate for your customers.

Request to fill a vacant position:

Status: Your request has been received and is approved.

Next Steps: Your request will be posted and we will send you the top 10 qualified applicants.

Approximate Timeline: The job will be posted for five days and we will send you qualified applicants in the three days that follow closing the posting.

Planned Outcome: You will receive the top 10 qualified candidates.

Complete SNAP Statement: Your request to fill the sales manager vacancy has been received and was approved. This opening will be posted within 24 hours and open for applicants for five days, after which we will send you the top 10 qualified candidates — usually within three business days after closing the posting to allow time for a resume review. Do you have any questions as we prepare to post this position?

(Note: For this example, there is more emphasis around the approximate timeline, as there are several steps that have specific time lines associated with them.)

Wait times at a restaurant:

Status: Welcome and thank you for choosing us for dinner this evening; we do have a short wait for a table.

Next Steps: Here is a pager; we will buzz you when your table is ready; in the meantime, please make yourself comfortable in our lounge.

Approximate Timeline: The wait for a table in the front room is about 45 minutes and for a table in the patio the wait is less than 30 minutes.

Planned Outcome: We will have your table ready.

Complete SNAP Statement: Welcome and thank you for choosing us for dinner this evening; we do have a short wait for a table. The wait for a table in the front room is about 45 minutes and for a table in the patio the wait is less than 30 minutes. Will that be OK? Great. Here is a pager, please make yourself comfortable in our lounge and we will buzz you when your table is ready.

(Note: In this example, the customer is asked if they are willing to wait for a table. If the customer is not willing to wait, then the next steps and planned outcome will not matter.)

Car repair:

Status: Your car is next in line; we are ahead of schedule today.

Next Steps: We will run a diagnostic, let you know what we find and with your approval complete the repairs.

Approximate Timeline: It will take two hours to run some tests; we will give you a call in two hours and let you know what we find.

Planned Outcome: After we run some tests, we will tell you what repairs your car needs.

Complete SNAP Statement: Thank you for choosing us today. Your car is next in line; we are ahead of schedule today. We will run a diagnosis, let you know what we find and with your approval complete the repairs. It will take two hours to run some tests; what is the best way for us to reach you in about two hours? So we can let you know what we find. After we run some tests, we will be able to tell you what repairs your car needs and get your approval to continue.

(Note: For this example, there is a need to know how to reach the customer in a short period of time, and the planned outcome at this stage is not the actual car repair but sharing the mechanic's findings and getting approval from the customer to proceed.)

Progress of a multistage project:

Status: We have completed stages 1 and 2 and are starting stage 3.

Next Steps: The work team will meet twice within the next week to discuss their findings for outlining stage 3.

Approximate Timeline: A draft of stage 3 will be completed two weeks from today.

Planned Outcome: With the completion of stage 3, the project will be completed and ready for submission to the Board for final approval.

Complete SNAP Statement: We have completed stages 1 and 2 and are beginning stage 3. The work team will meet twice within the next week to outline stage 3 with a final draft completed two weeks from today. The project will then be complete and ready for submission to the Board for approval. If you have any input, please get with me before next Friday.

(Note: In this example, the status part of the message contains a closure or planned outcome update related to stages 1 and 2, and then moves on to the timing of stage 3. The final planned outcome is not stage 3, but being ready for Board approval. This statement also asks for input and places a timeframe for that input.)

The status of a back order product:

Status: Your order has been successfully submitted and is currently on back order.

Next Steps: You will be notified via email when your order is filled; the email will include the shipping date and expected date of delivery; we will call to follow-up and make sure everything is all right with your purchase.

Approximate Timeline: Due to this product being on back order we do not have a fulfillment date; we will contact you in 10 days to give you an update regarding the back order status. Do you want to continue with your order for this product?

Planned Outcome: We will let you know when your product is available for shipment; we want you to enjoy this gadget with your new laptop.

Complete SNAP Statement: Your order was submitted and the laptop gadget is on back order. When the gadget is available, we will let you know the shipping and delivery date. Since the laptop gadget is on back order we don't yet have a fulfillment date; we will contact you in 10 days to give you an update. Do you want to continue with your order for this gadget?

(Note: A back ordered product statement is generally not about the product, but is more about the fact that the product is on backorder. This statement promises a follow-up within a specified time to update the customer about the back order. And, because of the back order, the customer is asked if they want to continue with their order.)

Adding a new dependent to insurance coverage:

Status: All your documents are complete, and have been successfully submitted to the insurance company.

Next Steps: The insurance company will review and process your request; you will receive a new health insurance card once your dependent has been added.

Approximate Timeline: It takes the insurance company about two weeks to do the initial processing; you can expect your dependent to show on your coverage within the next 30 days. The effective date is the beginning of next month.

Planned Outcome: Your dependent will then be covered under your insurance plan and will be able to present his/her insurance card for treatment.

Complete SNAP Statement: The paperwork to add your dependent has been submitted to the insurance company — you will receive a new health insurance card once your dependent has been added. It is expected that your dependent will show as added to your coverage within 30 days — with coverage effective at the beginning of the month. At that time, your dependent will then be covered under your insurance plan and will be able to present their insurance card for treatment.

(Note: For this example, the emphasis is on the successful submission of insurance documents, which is one type of planned outcome, and more importantly, reinforces the final planned outcome, which is not only coverage but the ability to access that coverage.)

Also, please note that for final SNAP statements the words status, next steps, approximate timeline, and planned outcome are not used prominently or as key words in the final statements. In our examples above, these words are not used at all.

What we have done is pretty simple. Draft out some notes for each of the four parts of SNAP then take those draft notes and put together a final, complete SNAP statement.

As the snap of taking a picture is the way for the photographer to put a final picture together that makes sense for the viewers, putting the four parts of SNAP together presents the customer with a complete picture of what is going on.

That's it. Put the picture together. Now, all you need to do is get started.

"Getting started is often the hardest part of making changes in your life, whether it's an exercise regimen, a personal growth plan, a diet, or a program to quit smoking. Because we already have so many reasons not to start in the back of our minds…"
…*from Today Matters, John C. Maxwell*

SNAP, at its most basic level, is just that simple. Draft out a short statement for each part of SNAP; then condense those statements and put them together into one seamless SNAP message. Yup, just that easy.

———————————

Is there power in letting your customers know what the status, next steps, approximate timeline and planned outcomes are for what you are doing for them?

Do you see how the four parts of SNAP integrate giving a complete message to your customer?

———————————

Part 3. Beyond the Basics

In this section, we help you understand how you can take SNAP beyond the basics. With some guidance and practice, you can easily become a SNAP master.

Profit in business comes from repeat customers, customers that boast about your project or service, and that bring friends with them.
— W. Edwards Deming

Restoring Full Service

The cover of the book proclaims a way to restore full service. What does this really mean?

Part of the SNAP inspiration comes from good, old fashioned U.S. of A. gas stations. Remember, we used to call them "service stations".

During the 1950s and 1960s, when you pulled into a service station to fuel your car you got full service. And, though the attendant did not know it, he was fully engaged with SNAP. Took me a while to get wrapped around this, but consider what happens when you pull into the full service station — 1950s style.

As you pull in, you drive over a hose that triggers a bell in the station. The attendant comes running out as you come to a stop near the gas pump. The attendant is at the driver side door; you don't even get out of the car — all you do is roll down your window. The attendant asks you how many gallons of gas you want or if you want a fill up. While the attendant fills your tank he checks your oil, your wiper fluid, cleans your windows and lets you know the air pressure in your tires. He may do more, as well.

The SNAP is not related to what the attendant does for you; it is related to how he does it; the attendant communicates with you by how he delivers service. You remain in your car while the attendant attends to your car. You see what he is doing all the time. He talks to you and lets you know what he finds and asks you if you need anything else. It doesn't matter how quick it takes for this service to be delivered to you. What does matter is that you are informed every step of the way.

In the example of the service station, the actions of the attendant are his SNAP. You, the customer, know the status of what he is doing, you know what the next steps are, you know what the approximate timeline is, and you know what the planned outcomes are. The attendant checks in with you as he performs his tasks. You are fully informed. In large part, the method of service delivery allows you to see what the attendant is doing, and this is a major part of how you get SNAPed. You see what is going on. You know what is going on.

The concept of full service for SNAP is not about the steps the service provider is taking, and is about how the service is delivered, the follow up, the communications. It is focused on what the customer needs or wants to know; and, on what the service provider wants or needs the customer to know. The messages we send using SNAP drive the full service component of the relationship.

Let's consider why this is so important. In the example of the full service station, the attendant is visible. His visibility was a key part of his SNAP message. In today's economy most of us are not that fully visible to our customer. Technology has added more variability to our visibility — at times making us feel more visible due to the easy of sending off a message, and, more often, making us less visible due to more services being provided long distance.

We work remotely. We use faxes, email, the Internet, computer systems, texts, tweets, and other less personal forms of interacting. Our modern methods of less personal communication put a burden on the communication aspects of SNAP. Assume less, communicate more.

As you can see, from what has been covered so far about SNAP, you realize SNAP does not care. Doesn't care how you do your job, or what your process steps are. SNAP just wants to be used, to be snapped into place. The more impersonal your relationship, the more you will want to insert SNAP messages into your workflows. This will add a much needed personal touch to what may otherwise be less than personal relationships.

The service station attendant demonstrated SNAP just by doing what he did; moving around the car, doing his tasks, asking you questions, letting you know what he found. All real time. Today, we have to do more. We have to go out of our way to insert SNAP. Better yet, insert SNAP as real time as possible. This will result in your customer experiencing full service. This is what you want.

Do you see how SNAP is just focused on sharing an important message, and does not interfere with or drive your workflows?

Can you get closer to full service by improving your customer communications?

Are you willing to use any necessary technique to move closer to delivering full service?

Assume Less & Real Time

Let's briefly cover two topics. In the last section, we mentioned that you should assume less and also SNAP in real time. Let's take a moment to explore each of these ideas.

Tom Hackett, university professor says: "As a professor in a graduate business school, my technically savvy students bring a bachelor's degree, life experience, and substantial business skills to the classroom and to their on-line communications. Using SNAP on a regular basis has helped me learn about my students' challenges and has improved their connection to the complex course material in change management, leadership, and business ethics."

Assume less. What does this mean?

A communication dilemma with routine processes is that as we work those routine processes over many months, perhaps years, we subconsciously think that others know as much about those processes as we do. This is especially true with repeat customers, and with internal customers. Please understand, this is very dangerous.

Of course, you and your team know your processes, each step, the next steps, the subtleties of timing, and other less than obvious nuances. Your customers do not appreciate these fine points about your workflows — nor do you want them to. You want them focused on the outcomes you deliver.

Think of Tom's business students. There is no need for those students to know the professor's workflow or processes. There is a critical need to keep those students — Tom's customers — focused on outcomes, Tom's outcomes he delivers as the professor, and, of course, the outcomes delivered by each student.

SNAP wants to be a core part of the outcomes message. That is what SNAP is all about. Do not use SNAP to educate others about the inner workings of your workflows. Do use SNAP to consistently connect your customer to the outcomes, the results you deliver.

So, do not assume that the customer knows what you know. In fact, assume they know less than you. Assume they know less than they know. Customers forget. Or, they remember how things worked years ago. Or, they recall the one occurrence that deviated from the norm. Your customers are not your workflow experts.

Assume less, and communicate more. Use SNAP as the way to consistently send a short, positive, outcomes focused message.

In several of the previous sections, you read the words real time.

Real time means: Do it now. Communicate now. Don't wait.

"People create success in their lives by focusing on today. It may sound trite, but today is the only time you have. It's too late for yesterday. And you can't depend on tomorrow. That's why today matters."
… *from Today Matters, John C. Maxwell*

Your relationship with your customers is happening now, it is happening today. This is why real time matters.

"As a language instructor, I not only teach language, but I have to make an extra effort to be clear in communicating with my students," says Katherine Espinosa, an English-Spanish language instructor working in Madrid, Spain.

She goes on to tell us, "Working with busy business men and women, I need to keep them informed basically in real time, so they can plan their schedules. This is also important to me since my income is dependent on my students. At the start of each learning session I let the student know the status for the learning session, what to expect next, how much time we will spend on a lesson and why we are doing it (the planned outcome). I also update [SNAP] my students at the end of the session to set up our next meeting, and to keep the student excited about what they will learn next. SNAP works in any language."

Real time is good for your customers and is good for you. Save time by being real time. Don't assume what your customers know or don't know: inform them. Keep your customers up to date as often as realistically possible. Connect with your customers. Treat each as an individual.

Do you see the danger in putting off customer follow-ups?

Can you be more productive by assuming less and making a point of sharing more with your customer?

Do you see the value in communicating now, moving to real time, and not keeping your customer waiting?

Objections

Perry Mason, the attorney character created by Earl Stanley Gardner, was noted for proclaiming, "Objection! Immaterial! Irrelevant! Incompetent!"

Younger readers might connect with the word objection shown in over sized red letters and shouted by Phoenix Wright.

Either way, when it comes to objections, they are all immaterial, irrelevant and incompetent! Exclamation point used with purpose and intent.

"A man cannot directly choose his circumstances, but he can choose his thoughts, and so indirectly…shape his circumstances."
…from As A Man Thinketh, James Allen

There are many reasons for not doing SNAP — or so others will tell you. I have been teaching others about SNAP (or a version of SNAP) for over 10 years. Objections to using SNAP (or some similar approach), can generally be traced back to how we choose to think — or choose to not think — about how we connect with customers.

Here are some of the more commonly mentioned reasons for not doing SNAP. Understand these and other objections and choose not to get stuck.

Read through these objections. Do any of them sound familiar; have you used one or more of these, or have you heard these types of objections from others?

I have heard these objections and many others over the years. The ones noted below are the most common. You will notice some of these objections sound redundant, however, there are subtle differences. Objectors will actively engage in nuances and shades of gray.

"I don't have enough time." This is my favorite. The person who says this is saying they don't have time for their customer. They are choosing to not connect with their customer. With some coaching, we can help this person know that taking time for the customer is critical to success; and, for the selfish person — the one who doesn't care that much about the customer — we can help them understand that using SNAP will actually save them time.

"It takes too long." It is true that doing something new will take some extra time. However, using SNAP in plug and play mode is almost effortless. As you use SNAP, and find that you have bought back time, you will have extra time to invest in making SNAP more effective for you. SNAP takes 30 to 60 seconds. Those who say it takes too long don't know what they are talking about; they are telling you they are not willing to invest in their (your) customers.

"I don't know what the status of things are." Well, if you don't know the status of things, then what does your customer know? This person is choosing not to know. You know more than your customer. Power users of SNAP will toss out multiple SNAP messages; this is especially true when the status is uncertain or changes quickly or frequently.

"Things change too fast for me to tell customers." Those who say this may be afraid to make simple decisions. Of course, things change. That does not mean we can't know what is happening now — in terms of status or timing. This person is choosing to avoid making a decision. Go ahead, and make a commitment, let your customer know what is going on — and if things truly change quickly, then promise your customer a follow-up SNAP. The amount of time it takes to do this is much less than the time it takes for you to react to customers and their questions.

"They already know, why tell them again." This is usually said of repeat customers or internal customers. They know what we do, so why take time to tell them? Whether you think your customers know what is going on or not, your work for them is still part of a workflow. This person is choosing to not make an extra effort. Add SNAPs into your workflows. Go ahead, tell them what they already know. The whole idea is to connect with your customers. If you are focused on connecting with customers, then so what if they know or think they know what you are doing for them. Go ahead and tell them with a careful, thoughtful, conversational SNAP.

"I'll do it; I save my SNAPs for the end of the day." This person is basically saying that they give up — other objections having failed, you will likely hear this one. Don't accept it. This is a bad compromise. Recall our earlier thoughts on real time. End of the day is not real time. Go for real time.

"I don't understand." This objection is from someone who does not want to take time to think. SNAP does not require hours and hours of thinking, it does take some investment, but that investment is easy to make. The person who says they don't understand may need your assistance to better understand who the customer is and how important the customer is to your business. If this person is an uncooperative employee, you may need to help them understand how important the customer is to their j-o-b.

"What difference does it make?" This person is similar to the prior one; they need to know how important the customer is. Perhaps you have an opportunity to align incentives. Usually employees or customer service providers who don't connect what they are doing to customer outcomes have some form of misaligned incentive. Help this person see the WIIFM — What's In It For Me?

As with objections about doing SNAP, you will find there are many objections about doing SNAP in real time. Some of these are:

"I am more productive batching my work. I will do my SNAPs all at the end of the day." When done properly, SNAP takes so little time that claims suggesting greater productivity can be achieved when not doing SNAP just don't make sense. Your customers are individuals. Treat them as individuals. Don't batch them. Though batching may work for processing transactions, SNAP is not a transaction, it is an important communication between you and your customer.

"I will do my SNAPs later, I am too busy now."
Your customer experiences are all one of a kind interactions. Even though you have a process to handle many customers, each customer wants and needs to be treated as though they were your only customer. SNAP takes such a short time to do there is no real reason to not communicate with your customer now. If you are connected to why you are doing SNAP in the first place, to improve service, and perhaps more importantly, to improve the perception of your already great service, then doing SNAP now just makes sense. Your customer is getting service now, so, SNAP the customer now.

"I can be more effective if I bundle similar customer interactions and then SNAP a bunch of customers all at the same time." This is bundling. It might work for transaction processing, however, this violated the concept of treating each customer as an individual. Do not send the same SNAP message to several customers at the same time. While you can be efficient by using a SNAP template, which can be customized — do make a point of customizing your message and sending or giving an individual message to each customer.

"A real sense of urgency is rare, much rarer than most people seem to think. Yet it is invaluable in a world that will not stand still. Complacency is pervasive, in part because it simply is not seen, even by many smart, experienced, and sophisticated people."
...from *A Sense of Urgency*, John P. Kotter

"I'll get to it tomorrow." This is one of the most dangerous objections. You may hear this objection, used not so much as an objection to the team, but actually said to the customer. And, yes, members of your team will actually say this to your customers. There are two big dangers with this objection. First, when the customer hears this, they hear confirmation that they are not valued. Understand this will result in lower customer satisfaction. I think you get that. Second, this confirms there is complacency in your team.

The people who use any of these, or other objections, are telling you they do not fully understand the WIIFM of the SNAP proposition — WIIFM = What's In It For Me.

"They will just ask more questions."

"It's too much information."

"If they really want to know, they will ask."

"It's a waste of time."

You will hear these and many other objections. Listen to them and respond with care. Objections are a way for the other person to tell you:

1. They don't get it.

2. They don't care; they are complacent.

3. They truly don't understand.

4. They are resisting; avoiding change.

5. They are not willing to make an effort.

6. They are not interested in improvement.

Use workshop opportunities to identify objections, the reasons for the objections and work through bringing others to a greater understanding of the importance of your customers.

When working SNAP with a team or small group, an excellent educational exercise is to hold small group discussions using these and other obstacles as topics. You will quickly know who gets it and who doesn't. Seeing these different positions with members of your team or your leaders, or your business partners, allows you to more easily hone in on any customer service communication gaps.

Gaps are opportunities for growth.

Make a point of discussing WIIFM with your team. You can do this by asking some questions focused of individual team members. Feel free to customize or add other questions based on your team, your industry or the specific WIIFM challenge you need to solve. Some questions to ask:

Have you ever struggled to get the customer to understand that you are really working on _____ (fill in the blank) for them?

Have you ever wondered why your customer's ask such silly questions?

Have you ever wished your customers would stop interrupting what you are doing so you can just get your work done?

Have you ever wished you had more time available to you during the day?

Have you ever wished your customers had a better understanding of what was going on with ___ (fill in the blank)?

Have you ever wished your customers saw you and your co-workers as a more integrated team?

Have you ever wondered what you can do to get better customer service scores?

These and other similar questions are great ones to use when working with your team or co-workers. Use them with yourself, as well. What can you do to improve your relationship with your customers? There are probably many options that will come to mind as these questions get answered.

One absolutely great, fantastic option is SNAP.

Insight: As you consider SNAP and work through objections, start by just looking at your use of time. Most likely you will find two things:

First: Objecting to and avoiding the use of SNAP takes more time than adopting SNAP. We all don't need to become level five masters. Avoiding the most basic use of SNAP takes more time than just using it.

Second: Not using SNAP and dealing with customer questions, research, investigations, follow-up, complaints, criticisms and less than desirable customer service scores all takes significantly more time than just pushing SNAP out of the box and doing a plug and play. Know that SNAP all by itself does not eliminate service failures or the need to deal with customer issues. However, it can dramatically reduce service failure occurrences.

Let's understand that many customer complaints are not related to errors, processes that break, products not delivered or service not performed. Too many are directly related to a gap in expectations. If you have investigated customer complaints, the worst ones to explain and correct for are those caused by expectation gaps.

"I do not believe in excuses. I believe in hard work as the prime solvent of life's problems."
Quote attributed to James Cash Penney, founder of J. C. Penney Company

While there are most certainly 10,000 reasons not to do something, focus on the one or two really good reasons out there to actually engage, initiate, implement.

"What a concept! I've often been frustrated with balancing the desire for constant updates on projects, yet challenged with not wanting to waste valuable time or provide unnecessary emails too soon before projects are completed. What a difference it's made by proactively applying this simple technique to diminish any concerns that all is being taken care of," says Monica Treacy, retail marketing consultant.

Be material! Be relevant! Be competent!

Use SNAP to attack the Gap. Be a doer. Make SNAP happen. Run past the objections as fast as possible and take others with you.

———————————

Are you able to identify and work through objections?

Do you see how objections are excuses to avoid change?

Are you willing to move past objections and focus on proactively delivering improved outcomes?

———————————

Why I Love McDonalds

A little bit more about the Gap.

Don't underestimate the Gap. This is why I love McDonalds. The world famous restaurant chain does not underestimate the Gap. They are all about the Gap. Everything they do is about the Gap. Let me explain.

Please understand, McDonalds does not serve up a gourmet dining experience. Their proposition is very different. Of course, they do have standards for their food items. If you go to any McDonalds, you will get (almost) the same food. In fact, it will be so similar and so "almost the same" as any other McDonalds that, for our purposes, it is the same.

Everything done by those who work at a McDonalds follows a strict set of processes and workflows. The food is assembled and prepared according to strict and predictable processes. Staff meets and greet customers with strict and predictable phrases and questions. These workflows result in highly predictable results.

Using consistency and predictability you can eliminate the customer Gap.

While I am not a McDonalds connoisseur, I have been to a McDonalds in 30 of our 50 states and in several other countries. My experience in each store was basically the same from one to the other. This is by design. This contributes to the predictability of the customer experience.

Please know I am not advocating for bland sameness. I am suggesting that one part of McDonalds' success is based on managing the customer experience through predictability. So, you might be thinking: What does this have to do with SNAP?

One way to drive customer satisfaction is to use predictability to meet your customer's expectations, or, to exceed their expectations.

Always keep in mind that the Gap is all about the customer's expectations. It is up to you to not only know this, but to do something about it.

SNAP messages are perfect for defining and driving expectations. Use them to deliver your version of predictability.

Watch what happens when you go to McDonalds. Watch the staff. Purposely look at their processes, even if you can only see some of them and portions of others from the customer side of the counter. Pay attention, because you can see and hear a lot. How can you transform some of what you observe into what you do with your SNAP messages?

Listen to their commercials carefully. Go beyond the catchy tunes or the flashy glitz. What is being said overtly? What is being implied? Most of these commercials are 30 or 60 seconds. You will see the same message or a very similar version of it over and over while watching a half hour TV show. Pay attention and you will see the messages are very clear and are all about setting and influencing your expectations. They assume you are or will be a customer.

Tease out ideas that you might use as you consider where and how to use SNAP. Every minute of every day, McDonalds is teaching you how to improve your customer service delivery.

Whether you like the food sold by McDonalds or not, the company is very focused on the customer experience, since the customer experience is good for their business. Face facts, most of us care about customers because customers are good for our business. You know this, I know this and our customers know this.

This is why I love McDonalds. They care about customers.

Like any good organization, internal processes can erode. Recent experiences at McDonalds have shown me that employees following the process at times fail to connect with the customer. Customer connection is so critical. Following the process is important; following the process and not connecting with the customer is failure.

Those who only follow processes can show they follow the process by checking off a list — their goal is to do the list check off. Their goal is not to connect with the customer. Customer expectations and customer satisfaction will not improve when we just check off a list.

There are many businesses that use SNAP-like approaches. Find them. Become a customer. Study them. It does not matter what industry vertical these businesses are in; customer service translates across verticals. Make notes. Listen to the words that are used. Of those words you hear, which ones can you use? Which ones do you, as a customer, connect with?

Go to Chick-fil-A. This franchise has mastered the core concepts presented by SNAP and the employees make a point of connecting with their customers. It is a pleasure to go to this business.

Dan T. Cathy, President and COO of Chick-fil-A says: "Regardless of titles and specific job responsibilities, I think all of us at Chick-fil-A are in customer service." He goes on to say: "We make every effort to treat each Chick-fil-A guest with genuine honor, dignity and respect as well as attempting to anticipate their needs…"
… *from thefranchisehound.com*

Anticipating needs and fulfilling those needs is a core part of the SNAP approach when it comes to setting and delivering on expectations.

Another great business to watch when it comes to core SNAP principles is Trader Joe's.

Earlier in this book a quote from Execution, The Discipline of Getting Things Done (Larry Blossidy and Ram Charan) speaks to the importance of staying focused on the needs of customers. Great SNAP messages are vehicles for getting informal, routine customer feedback. This feedback helps you with other SNAP messages and is key to connecting with your customers.

A major part of Trader Joe's service strategy centers on simple customer connections. Paul Orfalea writes on his web site that "… they just talk to their customers every day."

…from www.paulorfalea.com

SNAP is a simple method for doing just that. SNAP focuses on making the talk you have with your customers have some form of purpose and intent. However, no matter how you look at it, it is very simple.

Connect with your customers at a personal level; avoid doing the check off. Do make a connection.

And, that is why I love Chick-fil-A and Trader Joe's.

With your increased awareness of SNAP, do you see how other companies that excel in delivering customer service use similar strategies?

Are these strategies simple enough that you can commit to using them to improve a broad range of outcomes?

Do you see how predictability helps us set and then deliver on expectations?

SNAP'ED

SNAP'ED stands for: SNAP the Extended Dimension; using the extended dimension is one way to get a big step closer to mastery.

"Because we want to provide good service for our customers, we often promise more than we can deliver. In many cases, firms are promising things beyond what anyone has seen or experienced. ... We've raised their expectations too high, so we can't blame our customers for being unhappy when we don't keep our word."
... *from Customers For Life, Carl Sewell and Paul B. Brown*

What can we do to really manage these expectations?

So far, we have covered the basics of SNAP. There is also an Extended Dimension, which comes after you have used SNAP for a while. It is part of mastering SNAP. You will discover that simple SNAP statements can be mixed and matched, linked with other SNAP statements, used in a variety of sequences or combined in other ways to greatly extend your use of SNAP. More importantly, this will let you leverage your customer impact.

Here are several ways to push SNAP to the limit.

Preview the next SNAP. When you toss out a SNAP statement, include a preview of when a follow-up SNAP will take place. This approach is very effective with longer, or more complex workflows because those workflows will have several spots that are good and natural candidates for SNAP statements. Using follow-up SNAPs also works especially well with customer relationships that span longer periods of time. This gives you pre-set opportunities (commitments) for getting back to your customer. Keeping your customer informed is a great way to reinforce expectations, drive customer perception and improve your service levels.

SNAP when nothing has changed. The power here is in the act of SNAP, not in the new information. The power is in the act of connecting with your customer. This can be done with both short- or long-term customer relationships. If your customer is waiting five minutes for a sandwich or waiting 20 minutes for a table at a restaurant, a SNAP — even though nothing has changed — lets the customer know you still have them in mind and value them. If your customer relationship is longer, for example spanning several months, these SNAP statements become even more powerful. Our customers want to know they are valued, and that we continue to think of them.

Include the team. Include others on your team when you toss a SNAP to your customer. This can be done easily with SNAP messages that are emailed, since email is such a dynamic and real time way of communicating. For example, if you and I are members of the same team, you can send a SNAP message to one of our customers and include me, your teammate on the message. I then respond to all, meaning I reply so that the customer gets my response and in my note I make a point of saying what a great job you did. This is just one way of doing a reply. Also, use this approach to confirm a SNAP from a team member; for this to be effective, include the customer.

This tag teaming can be focused on any number of things, such as, confirming and / or talking up a team mate, your manager, your company, your product, the customer's purchase, the customer's choice regarding some aspect of their relationship with you or your company. Tag teaming also can be effectively aimed at addressing other concerns the customer might be experiencing or voicing.

Link one SNAP to another. This technique is simple enough. Use one statement to link or hook right into another. This can be done as noted above by tag teaming with a co-worker, and it can be done by tag teaming your own messages. An example of this might be using a standard SNAP message focused on status and next steps, and then following up with a message that contains a testimonial important to your customer. Or, your linked SNAP might contain information about resources, support groups or similar products. We see this happen very easily in the automated world with auto-responders. This can be easily adapted to more simple person-to-person communications and to one-on-one emailed follow-ups. Auto-responders are not needed for us to be effective with a technique like this.

SNAP in real time. Many customer interactions take place in real time, so SNAP should also happen in the here-and-now. For other process steps, you may have discretion in timing; however, when communicating with your customers, don't delay, move your SNAP to real time. Avoid end of day batching. Real time is particularly effective when your customer is right in front of you. SNAP now.

Include closing questions. Don't assume the relationship is either going well or is going to end well. Ask. At the end of your SNAP statement ask for feedback from your customer. Ask them if there is anything else they need. In the world of automation, with web based purchases and web based customer relationships you may have received a post action, emailed customer satisfaction survey. Using closing questions is not about doing a customer satisfaction survey. It is about staying focused on your immediate relationship and asking specifically if there is anything else needed, asking if the customer needs anything else as the immediate service is brought to completion.

Positive Answers. Another way to use closing questions is to purposefully ask questions to which the customer will give a positive answer. You are after a positive answer to positive aspects of the customer relationship, the product or your service. Your goal here is to get the customer to say yes. When the customer says yes they must choose to say yes and that means they are taking positive action, hearing themselves share a positive message — this reinforces for the customer that they have had a positive experience.

On occasion I have heard from others that they do not want to ask these types of questions, because they are not confident they will get a positive response from the customer. If this is truly the case, all the more reason to ask these questions. This is a strong clue you have opportunities.

Closing statements. In addition to using closing questions, use a closing statement. Share your basic, simple SNAP message, then close it with a strong and powerful aspect of the Extended Dimension. Tell your customer that you have fulfilled your commitment, met your part of the bargain, kept your promise, and delivered on the expectation. While this sounds very much like bragging about what you have done, what you are really doing is informing your customer. You are helping to support and manage key expectations that drive or form your customer's perception.

Repetition. Consider a key advertising principle. "Tell them what you are going to tell them; tell them; then, tell them what you told them." Watch or listen to any commercial on the TV or radio. You will hear a message that literally tells you what you are going to be told, you are then told the message and then you are told what you were just told. This is both simple and complex all at the same time. Meaning, it is simple to do, but difficult to get all the right pieces in the right places.

Why does this work? It works because, as customers, we don't work to understand what is going on. We accept what is going on at an intuitive or gut level. Think about your routine experiences when you are the customer. You don't study what is going on. It happens. You experience it. You accept it. You have expectations, and you want them met.

On the flip side, those providing the service or the product work very hard to make what is happening a great and meaningful experience for you. The provider works hard. The receiver does not.

As a service the provider, do your hard work. Extend your SNAP statements. Make some of them mini commercials. Advertise what you are doing, what you did, what you plan to do. As you use the Extended Dimension push yourself. SNAP statements can be short, to the point, and frequently shared mini commercials.

Undoubtedly, there are many other ways to extend your use of SNAP. Find them and use them. The ideas shared above are just a starting point.

- Preview when a follow-up SNAP will take place.

- SNAP even when nothing has changed.

- Include others on your team in the SNAP.

- Link one SNAP to another.

- SNAP in real time.

- Include closing questions.

- Ask questions that will get a positive answer from the customer.

- Use a closing statement.

- Use repetition.

Use the Extended Dimension of SNAP to leverage your customer relationships and significantly improve your service levels. When used consistently, with thought and purpose, you will find this is very powerful stuff.

Can you see the power of simple SNAP messages?

Can you imagine the increased power of extending your SNAP messages?

Reverse SNAP

SNAP is a powerful tool. Use it proactively to set expectations and consistently improve customer service.

Earlier in this book we briefly discussed those occasions when you wish you had seen or been on the receiving end of a SNAP message. Don't remain disappointed; be proactive and engage in a reverse SNAP.

A senior executive for a large international corporation was expressing frustration during a conversation with me earlier in the year. He was dealing with an interdepartmental issue, where another department was processing a transaction for him. The processing department did not communicate with the executive about the status of the action.

The timing of knowing the status of the transaction was important to him because it had implications for other members of his team, and he wanted to keep his team informed. After sending numerous emails the only response he received was, "Will let you know in a week or so."

We discussed his situation. In frustration, he said to me, "I just want to know what is going on. I need to keep my team informed." He purposely wanted to avoid using the power of his position to come down hard on the transactional department — though he could have.

We discussed various options, ranging from getting another senior officer involved to going to the support staff in the transaction area and calling them out. As a responsible leader, he then said, "I just need to know that they have had an opportunity to know what I need."

This is where we landed. Use SNAP. Toss out a reverse SNAP. For him, it went something like this:

"This is a follow-up to my request for [action] to be processed. It is important for me to keep my team informed. Please take a moment and let me know the status of processing this action, what the next steps are, your estimate of the approximate timeline to complete this action, and your thoughts on what the planned outcome is. If you have any questions, please let me know."

The statement above is rather comprehensive. It worked for this executive. He did get the information he needed. The reverse SNAP prompted the staffer processing the transaction to respond. There is a risk with tossing out the comprehensive reverse SNAP noted above. The risk is that it might overwhelm the receiver.

Move into your reverse SNAPs slowly. Start off by asking one or two simple questions. Simply ask some questions. Frequently, you will be a customer waiting for some feedback from others. This happens all too frequently when you are an internal customer waiting for a response from another co-worker or another department.

With reverse SNAPs it makes sense to specifically use the words status, next steps, approximate timeline and planned outcome. Use these SNAP words in your questions. You want to make sure there is no ambiguity or room for alternate interpretations of your questions. So, be specific, be simple, be right to the point.

Sample question statements are:

"Tomorrow is the deadline for X, can you please share the status and next steps with me."

"I understand that X is still in process, can you share with me the approximate timeline for completion of the next steps."

"Thanks for the update regarding X, what are the immediate next steps you plan to take?"

"Thanks for taking the time to work through the details of X, please share with me the anticipated planned outcome."

"Please let me know the anticipated timeline for completing X."

"Please let me know the status of X."

When using these types of questions, keep them simple. Don't ask about status, next steps, approximate timelines and planned outcomes all at one time. Do ask about one or two of these SNAP parts; asking about too much at one time may result in confusion.

As a smart, experienced SNAP user, you can easily address all four parts of SNAP. If you are working with others and you are compelled to send in a reverse SNAP question, you know that person is not an experienced SNAP user. So, keep your reverse SNAP questions simple and to the point.

Leverage your use of SNAP. Educate others.

Using reverse SNAP questions will also serve as a reminder for those who are new to SNAP.

Use reverse SNAP on a regular basis to reinforce team effectiveness and open up communications.

Use reverse SNAP on a regular basis to help others learn how to use SNAP.

Use reverse SNAP on a regular basis to set and reinforce expectations, and further drive customer satisfaction.

Take reverse SNAPs that you receive personally. They are a message that you have opportunities. Someone is telling you in clear language that you need to send him or her a SNAP. Be proactive and connect with your customer.

Can you see yourself using reverse SNAPs to get information you need as a customer?

Do you see how a reverse SNAP can help educate others?

Do you see how receiving a reverse SNAP is a message to you that you have opportunities?

Cautions

"Ninety-nine percent of the failures come from people who have the habit of making excuses."
... *attributed to George Washington Carver*

As you use SNAP use it with purpose and intent. Use it thoughtfully. And, make a point not to abuse SNAP.

You might be asking yourself how you could possibly abuse SNAP. Here are some ways.

SNAP is not an excuse machine. Do not use it to give excuses or updates on failures. There are other tools designed specifically around service recovery for these types of situations. This is beyond the scope of this book. Use SNAP to set and reinforce expectations, to provide updates that demonstrate fulfillment of expectations and to answer questions for the customer before the customer develops anxiety.

SNAP is not spam. Do not use SNAP messages in a way that mimics or simulates spam. It is not about how many times you share a message with your customer. It is about how you connect with your customer specifically about their current relationship with you.

SNAP is not an auto-responder. Avoid, at all costs, doing SNAP in a "check-off" fashion. If done this way, doing SNAP will be more harmful than helpful. It will highlight your lack of connection with the customer. Instead of guessing that he or she is not cared about, a check off approach will confirm to the customer that you do not care.

SNAP is not about frequency. It is about quality. Even though being consistent, constant and frequent (as dictated by your specific situations) are important concepts, it is critical to keep in mind that doing SNAP just to be consistent or just to be constant or just to be frequent is not sufficient. It is key to use those concepts to connect with your customer and to keep your customer focused on your relationship, to form and reinforce expectations and to share statements about your deliverable. You measure your success using a business metric or rubric — measurements will vary for each of us. You don't measure success by how many or often you SNAP.

SNAP is not about explaining your work process details. Your business is your business. Your customer wants a service or a product from you. Do not use SNAP to explain the inner workings of what you and your team do. Your customer does not care. They are not an expert on your workflows, your process, your machines, your equipment or your internal decision making process. So, don't use SNAP to involve them. Treat your customer with respect; respect their desire to get your service or your product.

SNAP is not about over explaining. Do not use SNAP to share blow-by-blow accounts of what you are doing. This is similar to the caution above, however I note it separately. I have noticed that less experienced workers who don't fully understand SNAP will use it to share minute by minute or day-by-day details and sequencing with a customer. Don't do this. The customer does not care. In fact, it is counter productive. It sends the wrong message to the customer. You want to send the customer positive messages related to expectations, what you are doing for them, preparing for them — you want to keep them focused on the prize, the outcome.

SNAP is not about you being a hero. It is about the customer.

SNAP is not an outcome. SNAP is a method to reach or deliver outcomes.

As you use SNAP, make a point of using it with purpose and intent. Remember these key points:

- SNAP is not an excuse machine.
- SNAP is not spam.
- SNAP is not an auto-responder.
- SNAP is not about frequency.
- SNAP is not about explaining your work process details.
- SNAP is not about over explaining.
- SNAP is not about you being a hero.
- SNAP is not an outcome.

Use SNAP to improve your customer's experience.

Can you see how the most effective use of SNAP is focusing on those things that are important to the customer?

Are you willing to avoid using SNAP to boost your ego, which distracts from your service outcomes?

Do you see the danger of auto-responding instead of using a custom SNAP message?

Mastery

"Part of surfing better and smarter is making a deliberate effort to improve. To maximize your surfing performance, pick one thing to work on every time you surf."

...from Surf Better, Dave Rearwin

Improve your service outcomes by making a deliberate effort to improve. Follow the surfer advice: Pick one thing to improve on each and every time you SNAP.

Zig Ziglar, author, motivational speaker and former salesman, is quoted as saying: "Statistics suggest that when customers complain, business owners and managers ought to get excited about it. The complaining customer represents a huge opportunity for more business."

We are not masters when we first use SNAP. It takes time and practice. Listen to your customers; what you hear from them will help you know where to focus your improvement efforts. Work on one thing at a time and seek improvement. Take the journey to full, level five mastery one step at a time.

"Customer share is now more important…than market share…Companies must also shift their focus from winning a single customer transaction to winning a lifetime of transactions…through brand loyalty and the kind of exceptional service that can be delivered only by a skilled, committed workforce"
…*from Business Process Outsourcing, Edward E. Lawler III, Dave Ulrich, Jac Fitz-Enz and James C. Madden V*

What does this mean to us? It means that every one of us, at all levels in the organization, have the burden and responsibility of supporting our brand and delivering exceptional service. Each and every time. Today.

Do this by mastering SNAP.

Mastery, Level One — Draft Three SNAP Messages. When you first use SNAP you will focus on simple messages. Know that simple messages are the core of SNAP. This first level of mastery is centered on those simple messages. To graduate level one, draft three SNAP messages that fit into one or more of your key and routine workflows. Your goal is to have three usable messages that can be used routinely within one of your key workflows. Do this during week one.

This level is the simplest and easiest level in terms of technical skill — yet is the most difficult because it is the first step on your change journey. Yes, embracing and using SNAP will require a change journey.

"...if we want to see change, we had better not wait [until later] for it to happen. How can we have hope in tomorrow if today is not different? ... Our action plan is what we do in the next hour. Not what we say, but what we [actually] do together."
...*from Flawless Consulting, Peter Block*

Level One is your call to begin the journey. Here and now. Not later. The call is now.

Mastery, Level Two — Use Three SNAP Messages Routinely. This second level is focused on the use of your first three messages. Your messages should be usable on a daily basis (or, at a minimum three times a week). If your messages are not routine enough for that level of usage, then go back to level one and develop messages that are part of a key and routine workflow. Use these messages for a minimum of three weeks. Your goal is to get a few simple SNAP messages into your daily practice, to develop a habit around SNAP usage. Developing this habit and a SNAP way of thinking is critical to long-term success.

At this level, you will begin to engage in daily disciplines that will set the foundation for long-term success with your customers.

Mastery, Level Three — Learn to Improve. At this level, you will master improvement. After getting past your first three weeks of usage, look closely and listen carefully to your messages and your customer's responses to them. Improve each message. Yes, that is correct, improve each of your three SNAP messages, and layer in additional messages. Target a minimum of three additional messages. Or, push yourself, and layer in five or more. Spend another three weeks at this level. During the three weeks improve each of your messages, your original three and the new ones you are layering in. The goal here is to reinforce the habit and pattern of SNAP usage, and, more importantly, to add in the habit of improving your messages and using new ones. An effective way to work through this level is to build a library of SNAP messages and message templates that can be customized. Focus on getting yourself prepped for level four.

At this level, you will also begin to think very differently about how you draft and complete your SNAP statements. Focus on being simple and concise.

"Do less, not more, but achieve more because of [these] choices... Simplicity boils down to two steps: 1) Identify the essential [and] 2) Eliminate the rest."
...*from The Power of Less, Leo Babauta*

Mastery, Level Four — Reach for the Extended Dimension. At this level, you are routinely using SNAP messages, you are improving ones that you generate, and you now are layering in ideas covered in SNAP'ED, Extended Dimension. You have a sufficient number of messages in your library, and have developed the ability to quickly put together and customize messages, and are now focusing on linking messages, including closing questions and closing statements. You are also looking more closely at your workflows to ensure SNAP messages are being used at the most strategic and opportune times. You continue to use the skills mastered during the previous levels.

At this level, you are now focused on value. SNAP messages are not about marking items off your checklist. If you are marking SNAPs off a list as you deliver them — such as, "Yup, tossed out SNAP number five just now. Five is good. My manager will love me. Five SNAPs in one day!" — then you are missing the core, fundamental reason for doing SNAPs in the first place.

At this level, you must be well past the routines of lower levels, where those routines were used to build discipline based on repetition. Focus on value.

"Since value is defined by the receiver, not the giver, any value proposition begins with a focus on receivers, not givers."
...*from The HR Value Proposition, Dave Ulrich and Wayne Brockbank*

Review your library of SNAP messages and make sure they are truly focused on value — that which your customer values.

Mastery, Level Five — Teach SNAP to Others. At this fifth level, you routinely: use SNAP messages; develop messages real time; access a library of simple and extended messages; customize simple messages to meet unique circumstances or individual customer circumstances; use closing questions to get customer feedback; use closing statements to reinforce expectations; and, improve messages as you use them. Your messages are focused on value and outcomes. And, to be a full level five SNAP master, you teach others to master SNAP, coaching and assisting three others to reach level four.

Begin small, keep it simple. Know that the power of SNAP comes from the consistent use of simple SNAP messages. The advanced levels of SNAP mastery are all based on leveraging these simple, core messages. Accept the challenge and become a SNAP MASTER!

Mastery, Level One — Draft and use three SNAP messages. One week.

Mastery, Level Two — Use your three SNAP messages daily for three weeks.

Mastery, Level Three — Improve each of your three messages and add three or more new messages. Do this over a three week period. Use this time to build up your library. Focus on discipline over routine.

Mastery, Level Four — Put the Extended Dimension into your messages. Improve your messages to focus on outcomes and adding value. Continuous improvement.

Mastery, Level Five — Teach SNAP to others. Coach and assist three others to reach level four.

SNAP can be trained in a workshop setting or one on one. The next few sections contain ideas about educating yourself and others on SNAP.

Can you see how your customers will gain value as you continue to use and improve your use of SNAP?

Are you willing to move from basic usage to mastery?

SNAP Out of It

"SNAP is a great framework for communicating any type of feedback or expectation. It has changed the way I communicate with my clients and colleagues," reports Kevin Hurlahe, Tae Kwon Do master instructor and President of Martial Arts Centers, Inc. He adds, "The uses of SNAP messages are truly unlimited!"

Running his own business, with a highly discretionary clientele, Master Kevin and his team pay very close attention to their customers. SNAP is not only a way of sharing a simple, single message, it forms a broader framework for keeping the customer engaged, and more importantly, keeping the customer returning. His business growth is largely based on personal referrals — this means that current customers are extremely important; they are the current business foundation and they are the source of the business's future.

Master Kevin goes on to share with us:

"SNAP is the overarching system we use to lead our students (customers) on their journey from white belts to black belts. Their Status is their current level of proficiency, for example, being at the White Belt level.

Their Next Steps are the specific skills they need to learn in order to earn their next level of proficiency (e.g. Yellow Belt). The Approximate Timeline is attending 30 classes at their current level to learn the required skills. Finally, the Planned Outcome is the attainment of the next level of proficiency — the graduation to Yellow Belt! At this point, the SNAP system restarts automatically and repeats itself through each belt level all the way to Black Belt.

"Moreover, within each of the belt levels there are intermediate SNAP stages along the way to keep each customer (student) on track, motivated, and informed about progress and expectations. For example, during the 30 classes of instruction between belt levels, students earn stripes on their belts at 10 and 20 classes. They also earn 'skill stripes' and merit patches to indicate the mastery of their skills at each level. This layering of SNAP systems and statements around continual feedback between the instructor and students creates a constant feedback loop so customers (students) always feel SNAP'ed about their relationship with us!"

In the beginning of the last section, Mastery, a quote about surfing from Dave Rearwin was shared: focus on one thing, practice it, perfect it. During workout sessions led by Master Kevin and his team, students focus on one thing and practice it over and over and over. During these sessions, the instructors use the SNAP technique setting expectations for students about the workout session, and then SNAPping on a routine basis — providing feedback to the class and to each student about their status, about next steps, about the approximate amount of time dedicated to the session and about the planned outcome.

If something changes during the session, if a student needs extra attention, if the instructors see the class needs a break, or if a minor injury needs to be taken care of, the use of simple, to the point SNAP messages resets the class's expectations — and keeps them informed.

Master Kevin goes on to tell us, "As our customers (students) encounter individual challenges or barriers to learning their individual skills, I implement SNAP, helping them from being discouraged, keeping them on track, motivated, and engaged in our programs. Now, when I see that someone is struggling with a concept or technique, or dealing with their own physical limitations or mental frustration over any part of their learning, I can immediately 'Snap them out of it!'"

As you master SNAP, know that it is designed to serve as part of your communication approach. However, also know, from the example shared by Master Kevin, you can choose to not only master SNAP as a communication technique, you can choose to use it as core to your business foundation. Where relationships with customers are absolutely critical, having a foundation based on customer communication is a strategy for success.

Are customers critical to your business success?

Is communicating with your customers so important that you are willing to do anything to keep them informed?

Are your current customer relationships important to future business?

What are you doing to engage customers today and how is that connected to the customers you plan to have tomorrow?

Part 4. Learning

In this section, we provide insights that will help you get SNAP up and running quickly for yourself, and also help you help others. Sample workshop outlines and other resources are provided for your use.

> *Be a yardstick of quality. Some people aren't used to an environment where excellence is expected.*
> *— Steve Jobs*

Why Workshop?

"In a global economy, nothing matters more than service. You might have hundreds, even thousands, of competitors—and that means your customers have hundreds, even thousands, of alternatives to doing business with you. Ultimately, the way customers are treated will make or break an organization."
...*from Results That Last, Quint Studer*

SNAP is simple and easy.

Perhaps, too simple and too easy.

A senior director I worked with several years ago planned out several SNAP sharing opportunities for his team. He presented the concept. He asked for feedback. He asked if the team was committed to improving customer service. The members of his team all responded saying that they thought using SNAP was a great idea. They all said that they were committed to improving customer service.

This director was excited about the feedback he received from his team. He and I discussed this as an excellent start one day over lunch.

Share the idea or concept with your team, and most likely — with most average teams — there will be understanding and acceptance. Of course, you will most likely hear your team say, SNAP just makes sense. Let's do it!

A little while later I checked in with him. Several weeks had gone by. I asked if he was still using the SNAP technique. He looked crestfallen as he replied. I learned that he was still interested in the concept, and though his team had expressed acceptance during their training sessions, no one on the team was using the technique.

Check back with your team a week later, or a month later. You might be surprised to find that SNAP is not being used. If it made sense when first shared, then why is SNAP not being used?

Are you and your team really willing to invest in change to embrace SNAP? Are you willing to focus on exceptional service? Are you willing to add SNAP into your service delivery tool kit? Are you willing, here and now, to do this, even though it is new or different from what you are currently doing?

Doing something different requires change. Change is linked to discomfort — change moves us away from the comfort of what is most familiar to us. We don't do what is best for us, we do what is most familiar. Whatever is most familiar to each of us is usually driven by our past practice — which has turned into our current set of habits.

So, getting SNAP into use is a matter of changing habits. Actually, it is a matter of choosing to understand the need to change a habit and choosing to act on that understanding. Don't kid yourself, this is not easy. SNAP is easy, but, changing habits is not easy.

Developing a habit, for example, the habit of using SNAP, requires purposeful practice.

"Habits are formed by consciously practicing certain actions repetitively, over a period of time. It takes *practice* and *time lapse* for [habits] to be formed."
...*from When Good Isn't Good Enough, Ron Willingham*

A popular myth suggests that it takes 21 days to form a habit, or, 21 days to break a habit. More current research suggests that habits are strongly linked to some form of reward — sometimes it is a reward we are aware of and, at other times, it is a reward of which we may not be consciously aware. We just know we do what we do. We might be avoiding pain, avoiding something uncomfortable, or avoiding the unknown. We might be moving towards something comfortable, something easy or, more likely, something we know.

Have you ever heard the statement: "That's just the way we do it." Maybe another version: "We have always done it that way." When people say this they are saying they are comfortable repeating a pattern of behavior without thinking about better ways of doing things. The subconscious reward might be ease of use (something we know), predictability (more stuff we know), or a reduced need to think (staying with what we know).

All too often we don't take time to think these patterns through, so we continue to repeat patterns of behavior that might have worked at some time in the past — but fail us today.

Things change. Our competition changes. Our customer's expectations change. The economic reality in our communities, our states, our regions and the places where we work changes. We don't have to like the fact that things change, but, we do have to know that to remain relevant we also need to change. SNAP is so powerful when used consistently, because SNAP messages can be adjusted, edited and customized quickly, on the fly.

Understanding this and choosing to use SNAP is the first step. Next steps can be shared during SNAP training.

Consider running a SNAP training series. Covering SNAP once and hoping all will be good, generally, will not be sufficient. A series of sessions will allow you to introduce SNAP, personalize it for each team member, reinforce key WIIFMs, and draft real world examples. Best results come from covering this over the course of several sessions, and not trying to cover everything all at once, hoping for change.

———————————

Can you clearly state why using SNAP will help you?

Can you clearly state why using SNAP will benefit your customers?

Do you really want improved customer service and improved business outcomes?

Are you able to share these reason with others?

———————————

Workshop Options

Get your team up to speed with SNAP. One approach to training SNAP is shared here. Feel free to customize based on your needs, the needs of your team and the challenges of your market sector.

Consider these types of questions. You should be able to answer these questions either before you conduct training, as part of your pre-training plan; or, answer these questions as part of your training program.

Define your why. Why is connecting with the customer important?

Find opportunities. What and where are the opportunities for you to connect with your customers?

What is working well today?

What is not working well today?

What can be improved?

What can you stop doing?

After improvement, what will success look like?

How will you measure success?

Here is a sample outline for a series of SNAP training sessions:

1. Introduce SNAP
2. Determine what is important to your customers
3. Identify why and how SNAP is important to your business
4. Personalize what SNAP means for each team member
5. Develop personalized WIIFMs for each team member
6. List out key workflows
7. Identify in each workflow where one or more SNAPs can be snapped
8. Draft SNAPs for workflows used by the work group
9. Customize SNAPs for each team member
10. Commit to using SNAPs
11. Practice using SNAPs
12. Draft a daily commitment grid (track and report)
13. Conduct a SNAP audit
14. Review and improve SNAPs

Structuring a set of training sessions is not difficult. There are a number of configurations that you can use. Choosing an approach that fits your team's schedule and work setting is best.

This content, and additional topics that are important to your industry or market, can be delivered in several ways.

1. An all day workshop.

2. Two half-day workshops.

3. Several two to three hour workshops.

4. Five to nine half-hour to one hour sessions. If you have the time to work on SNAP step by step, this approach is the most effective.

While I usually recommend multiple sessions, this is not always possible. Content from the outline shared above can be covered in one session, preferably a half-day minimum. Or, deliver content over three to nine sessions. Again, choose that which best fits how you and your team work.

The next section, Workshop Rhythm, will help you with the mechanics of structuring your training sessions.

Will SNAP training help you and your team?

Are you willing to invest in your team?

Workshop Rhythm

While you are, of course, free to structure your workshops any way you choose, and some of you might be instructional designers, many of us are average business people, so the following insight should be of use.

Consider structuring your workshop using a rhythm or pattern. Incorporate key adult learning principles, and set some goals.

Here is a sample rhythm:

- Introduce content / concept
- Keep the concept focused
- Share a scenario with the learning group
- The scenario may show either appropriate or inappropriate approaches, or a mix
- Lead a group critique of the scenario
- Share case studies
- Facilitate break out sessions for the learning group

- During these sessions small groups respond to, react to, or resolve the issue presented in the case study
- After a set period of time, each small group reports out to the larger learning group
- Discuss shared insights, identify gaps, discuss different perspectives

There are several major components in the rhythm listed above:

1. Concept
2. Scenario
3. Case study / Question
4. Workshop
5. Report Out

These components can be repeated or mixed and matched in many different ways.

As the learning group facilitator, you may need to determine if a particular concept must be repeated. If your students don't seem to get it, if you sense they don't understand, then repeating portions of a rhythm should be done. In your preparation for teaching others about SNAP you will have developed or gathered information related to several different scenarios and several different case studies for each concept. If you need to go into more detail, you will then have material that lets you extend practice without re-using the previous same examples.

If your training program spans several workshop sessions over the course of multiple days, begin each subsequent day with a review of what was covered before.

Build in question and answer sessions. A good rule of thumb is that if your students don't have many questions, they may not really connect with what you are teaching them. A good student, who understands the content, will always have questions. If your students don't appear to have spontaneous questions, break them into groups and give each group a mini-topic to discuss. Ask them, if they were sharing this with others, what questions would they anticipate others to ask of them.

At the start of this section we mentioned adult learning principles. Most adults will respond positively to problem-based, solution oriented and collaborative approaches — rather than didactic, top down, class room styles.

Consider yourself a facilitator, rather than a stand-up teacher — this allows for the perception of equality between the facilitator (teacher) and learner. Know that there may be adult learners in your group who have a greater connection with the subject matter than you —

your goal is to be prepared for this and to leverage this as you facilitate your learning group.

As you prepare your content, keep these other key aspects in mind: Your adult learners are self-motivated and self-directed; they bring a wealth of life and professional experience to the learning dynamic; they are goal and relevancy oriented; they will need to see the practicality of SNAP and how it applies to their specific circumstance; and, above all, adult learners must be respected.

While the above sounds like a long list, it can be summarized as:

1. Keep it real.
2. Understand your audience.

To make sure you get traction with your workshop, prepare your material in several ways. Include:

- Written materials
- Audio/visual materials
- Short facilitator presentations
- Group interaction
- Report out opportunities
- Participation opportunities for each learner
- Group mini-presentations
- Brainstorming

- Content improvement feedback
- Question and answer sessions
- Learner to learner assist (where a learner mentors or assists another learner)
- Games
- Quizzes
- Rewards for participation
- And, a favorite — a getting to know the other learners icebreaker.

(I use the word favorite above because, in my experience, icebreakers are not something most people like doing, but once done, most say it was very important in understanding the broader context of how the learning gets applied across the company, and, more importantly, helps them see different perspectives.)

Promote involvement with your class. A benefit "...of involving adults in activities is to increase retention. ...think back on some of the lessons you learned and still remember from the classroom; I have a sneaking suspicion there was an activity run around that lesson. There is an old saying that goes something like this: What people hear, they forget. What people see, they remember. What people do, they learn."
...from How To Run Seminars & Workshops, Robert L. Jolles

Think back to a prior section of this book, Mastery, moving from one level to another is all focused on doing. As you share SNAP with others, move as quickly as you can from talking about the concept to using the technique.

This book on SNAP is not dedicated to training methods and approaches. Hopefully, this section gives you a starting point. There are many other excellent resources that you can consult.

Continued use and practice is the best way to learn and master SNAP. This forms the most important rhythm as you deploy SNAP, for yourself and for your team.

Quick Start

Get started now.

"I have been impressed with the urgency of doing. Knowing is not enough; we must apply. Being willing is not enough; we must do."
...attributed to Leonardo da Vinci

Here are three steps you can do right now. Take these simple steps and get started with your SNAP messages; there is no time like now.

1. Write down three or four of your most routine, daily customer interactions. When do you interact with customers? What do you interact with customers about? Make sure these are daily customer interactions. Write these things down.

2. What questions do your customers ask during these routine interactions? What do they ask when they first get with you to initiate service? What do they ask later? What do they want to know? What do you want your customers to know? List out these things.

3. Write down how you answer or would like to answer these questions. Write down what you want your customers to know. Write down what you want your customers to know when service begins, during the course of service and when service ends. Write these things down.

Now, do your SNAPs. Moving through the three steps above will give you plenty of opportunities for drafting out your first three SNAP messages.

Pick one of the examples you noted. Then for that one item, move quickly:

1. Draft out a sentence addressing status.

2. Draft out a sentence addressing next steps.

3. Draft out a sentence addressing the approximate timeline.

4. Draft out a sentence addressing the planned outcome.

5. Now, combine these draft sentences; then edit to smooth out what you just wrote.

6. Read it out loud. Have someone listen from the customer's perspective.

7. Answer some simple questions: Does it make sense? Does it work?

You are now just a few minutes away from completing Level One of SNAP mastery.

Refer back to Part 2 Put It All Together. This will help you take action as you begin your SNAP journey. Refer to the samples of completed SNAP messages shared earlier. Remember, your customers want to know the status of things, what will happen next, how long things will take, and what will be done, the planned outcome.

"Staying connected to my customers is critical," says Jeremy Kuhne, small business gun shop owner. "Most of my business is based on how well I treat each customer, how well I keep them informed of a sale, a trade or special work I may be doing for them. I rely on each customer to come back and to refer me to new customers."

Get started now.

Measure Your Progress

Use this list to check up on your progress and to support your development and mastery of SNAP. Also, use this with others you guide along the SNAP journey.

Answer each question. Most questions can be answered with a simple yes/no; feel free to add an additional short answer where that helps you understand your progress. This checklist is not a test; it is a way for you to understand your SNAP journey and to rapidly engage in the use of SNAP.

Use this check list on a periodic basis, every two weeks is recommended for a fully engaged SNAP user, to measure and track your progress.

Do you know what the acronym SNAP stands for?

What does the "S" in SNAP mean to you personally?

What does the "N" in SNAP mean to you personally?

What does the "A" in SNAP mean to you personally?

What does the "P" in SNAP mean to you personally?

Have you listed out three or four key workflows?

Did you write out three basic SNAP messages that fit into your key, routine workflows?

Did you write out more than one version of each of these three basic messages?

Have you embarked on the SNAP journey?

Are you committed to using SNAP to improve your customer experience?

Are you committed to using SNAP to improve yourself professionally?

Do you use your three basic SNAP messages on a daily basis?

Are you preparing yourself to use these messages for a minimum of three weeks?

Are you listening to your customer's as you use your SNAP messages?

Are you looking for opportunities to improve your SNAP messages?

Have you improved each of your first three SNAP messages?

Have you drafted an additional three SNAP messages?

Are you pushing yourself to draft out another set of messages?

After improving your SNAP messages, are you listening to your customers in a whole new way?

Are you writing SNAP messages that blend into your normal and routine communication with your customers?

Are you continuing to use SNAP messages on a daily basis?

Are you focusing on setting expectations, moving beyond mere follow-up?

Are you looking for additional opportunities where you can use SNAP messages?

Are you drafting more and more messages, building up a library of messages?

Are you editing your SNAP messages on a recurring basis, pushing for simplicity and effectiveness?

Are you avoiding a check off approach to SNAP?

Are you writing and delivering SNAP messages with purpose and intent?

Have you identified a number of other key workflows where you can layer in SNAP messages?

Are you extending your use of SNAP messages, using key concepts from the SNAP'ED section of this book?

Are you continuing to build your SNAP library, giving you and your team flexibility when it comes to restoring full service?

Are you able to quickly customize messages, on the fly, real time?

Are you willing to continue your commitment to using SNAP to improve your business and yourself professionally?

Are you linking SNAP messages, in order to leverage the content of a message across a team?

Are you managing up your team's SNAP messages?

Are you managing up your customer?

Are you managing up your company's product or service?

Are you continuing to listen to your customer?

Are you harvesting (gathering) customer input in such a way it helps you shape expectations or deal with issues you did not anticipate?

Are you using this learning to improve your SNAP messages?

Are you focused on value?

Do you know what the customer values?

Are you using SNAP messages to reinforce what the customer values?

Are you using closing questions in your SNAP messages?

Are you asking for and encouraging customer feedback in such a way that the customer reinforces their satisfaction with your service or product?

Do you and your team have SNAP conversations at team meetings?

Are members of your team pushing each other to improve their use of SNAP?

Are you ready to be a SNAP Master?

Have you shared SNAP with others?

50 SNAPs

There are so many times, places, opportunities for us to use SNAP. There are only 24 in this list of 50. We need to hear from you. Please share your examples of where and when a good SNAP message can be effectively used.

You can do this easily by going to the snapthegap website and submitting your idea using the web form on that page (www.snapthegap.com/ideas).

These ideas might help you see opportunities in your work area, or, might spark ideas that assist you with educating others on the use of SNAP.

1.   Respond to the manager who requests a vacant job be filled.
2.   Respond to the job applicant who wants to work for you.
3.   Communicate with the customer who just ordered a burger.
4.   Respond to your boss who just requested an updated report.
5.   Communicate to employees and their families about changes in benefits plans.

6. Share with your customer who leaves their car to have brakes repaired.

7. Inform the IT steering committee regarding a go-live date.

8. Share awareness with users regarding changes to the look of their favorite software.

9. Connect back with volunteers even when there are no immediate needs.

10. Communicate with students on their progress on a project.

11. Add understanding to the software customer who doesn't understand why development is taking so long.

12. Keep family members of patients informed on the status of a surgery.

13. Connect as a volunteer with the organization about your challenges and progress.

14. Share with your vendors what you like/dislike about their work on your behalf.

15. Provide feedback to editors of the secular press and professional journals about articles and ideas presented.

16. Advise meeting facilitators how you are proceeding on assignments.

17. Communicate to the restaurant manager about the service, food, and drink you received.

18. Let patients and families in Emergency waiting room know about updates to wait times.

19. Update clients waiting for delivery of a new automobile.

20. Let customers know about the delivery of a package or mailed item.

21. Share the timing of a home inspection and what you need from your client.

22. Give a realistic preview of auto repairs with an estimate of timing and costs.

23. Give an update about repairs to customers waiting to assure them repairs are proceeding as planned.

24. Provide expectations to your students about the timing of course material and next steps during the semester.

25.

26.

27.

28.

29.

30.

31.

32.

33.

34.

35.

36.

37.

38.

39.

40.

41.

42.

43.

44.

45.

46.

47.

48.

49.

50.

Help spread the word about SNAP; share your ideas by going to the SNAP website at snapthegap.com/ideas.

Key Concepts

This is a resource section in which key concepts are listed and briefly defined. Consider these concepts as you implement and master SNAP. These concepts are described and defined within the context of SNAP.

Adult Learning
Use key adult learning principles when teaching others about SNAP. Key here is to keep learning sessions practical, show respect for your audience and provide participation opportunities.

Communicating
Letting your customer know what to expect. Done by taking the initiative to share a deliberate and structured message or set of messages with your customer. The sharing of SNAP statements.

Consistency
Managing expectations by sharing a message on a predictable schedule. Using workflow routines. Avoiding the treatment of customer interactions as exceptions.

Customer

The person who allows your business to thrive. Customers may be internal to your organization: someone in another department who depends on you so they can sell products or services to those who pay you or your company money. We generally think of customers as external to the organization: someone who pays you or your company money for products or services.

Customization

Adjusting your message to fit the needs or situation of a particular customer experience. Customization does not violate the concepts of consistency, routine or predictability.

Exceptions

Events or occurrences that deviate from the norm or violate a normal, routine workflow. While exceptions can be expected, they should not be routine and workflows and processes should be adjusted to reduce exceptions. Exceptions are a major contributor to errors.

Expectations

What one expects to see, get or experience. For us expectations are the standards of service we want to deliver, and most importantly, the service levels we want our customers to expect. SNAP is a way to set and manage the customer's expectations.

Frequency

Use SNAP regularly and routinely. Frequency is important to SNAP; use SNAP on a consistent and routine basis to set, reinforce and remind customers about expectations. Make deliberate decisions about the frequency with which you use SNAP. Too often may be dilute the impact; not enough and your customers will feel like you don't remember them.

Full Service

Treating each customer as an individual and using SNAP to set and manage expectations and to fully engage the customer.

Gap

The gap is the difference between what a customer expects, their expectations, and what they get, or more accurately, what they perceive they get. When we manage the gap, we strive to align perception with expectations. No matter how great our service levels, if there is a gap, the service we provide is perceived as less than satisfactory.

Implementation

To begin something by taking action. While planning and deliberation are important steps, making something happen by implementing a set of action steps is critical to success. For SNAP users, implementation happens when you actually begin to use SNAP.

Initiative

To have the courage to take action; to take action and to implement use of SNAP. See "implementation".

Investment

What you have to put into something in order to get something back. We are familiar with the idea of investing money in a money market certificate in order to get a return on our investment, more money back as some later date. For SNAP to work you need to invest yourself, some time and a little creative thought. You also need to invest time in listening to and understanding your customer. As with any good investment, your return on a SNAP investment will largely depend on what you choose to invest.

Link

Use one SNAP statement to lead to and support another. Deliberately link them together. Use the second one to leverage, support, and reinforce the first. Follow-up supporting messages are extremely powerful.

Mastery

Gained by investing time to improve your use of SNAP from level one to level five. Personal mastery comes from following a path of learning, use and practice. Layer on intentional improvement and sharing — teaching others.

Next

Help the customer know or connect with what will happen next. This is the strongest part of setting expectations. What happens next may be something you do or something your customer needs to do.

Objections

Reasons, usually not valid, for opposing or not using SNAP. Those who persist in objecting are telling you and others they don't care about the customer and are not interested in self development or improvement. Those who object are probably not connected to the mission of the business.

Out of the Box

A product, tool or technique that can be used without the need to assemble, construct of highly customize. SNAP is available out of the box. You can draft a SNAP message almost immediately — review the parts of SNAP and then use it.

Outcomes

Things that are to be delivered, or things that are to be done. Your customer is yours because of outcomes they want or believe you can deliver. SNAP connects where you are now with the customer's expectations around desired or anticipated outcomes. Use SNAP to align your understanding of outcomes with that of your customer.

Perception

That which the customer believes to be true. This is the most important part of your customer relationship management experience. SNAP is an extraordinarily powerful way for you to set, manage and influence customer perception. When your customer's perception does not match yours or what you are doing you then have a gap. Having a gap is not good.

Plug and Play

A device is said to be plug and play when you unpack it, plug it in and turn it on. SNAP is plug and play, since all you need to do is unpack it, plug it into a workflow and let it play. See "out of the box".

Practice

Use SNAP as often as possible. Use results in improvement, better SNAP messages and improved relationships with your customers.

Predictability

Using SNAP to meet predefined expectations. SNAPs are predictable because you set the expectation regarding the use of SNAPs and other defined and predicted service delivery. Predictability gives your customer ease and assurance.

Preview

To give the customer a hint of something yet to come. Use SNAP to preview the coming of other

SNAPs, and more importantly, to let the customer know about planned outcomes.

Process

A collection of workflow steps, together called a process.

Real Time

To the greatest extent, do things now. Don't line them up for later. Your customer is interested in an outcome in real time. They want something now. Even if they are waiting for delivery, they want something now. So, get into real time and connect with your customer now.

Repetition

Develop SNAP statements that repeat core messages that are important to your customer relationship. Repetition should not be mindless, however, it should reinforce.

Review

To look closely at your SNAP statements and to improve them. Invest time to make your statements better.

Status

The first part of a SNAP statement. Let the customer know something important about the status of their relationship with you.

Timeline

The third part of a SNAP statement, approximate timeline. Let the customer know when things are scheduled or expected to happen.

WIIFM

Stands for What's In It For Me. To get buy in from others on new ideas or changes to how the team works it is best to help those who will be changing to understand why it is good for them to adopt the change. For SNAP to succeed help your team connect with their WIIFM.

Workflow

See process. A workflow is a collection of steps that moves an action from inception to completion. Plug your SNAP statements into key parts of your workflow.

Workshop Rhythm

Structure an effective workshop using these high level components to set a pattern or rhythm: Share concept; present and critique scenarios; and, work through case studies.

Part 5. Closing

Thank you for taking time to read about SNAP.

In this section, we summarize what has been presented and thank those who provided input and assistance in the writing of this book.

*Do what you do so well that they will want to see it
again and bring their friends.*
— Walt Disney

Stuck?

You might get to a point where you feel stuck. That is normal.

I have been using and sharing the concept of SNAP with others for more than ten years. I still get stuck. The best way to get past being stuck is to talk to someone else.

Share with them what you are stuck on. Ask for ideas, insights, thoughts, options, examples, alternatives — you get the idea. The idea is to get more ideas. To get someone else to help you see a different way to:

- Say something
- Describe something
- Combine the parts of SNAP
- View your workflows
- Listen to your customer
- Set expectations
- Understand outcomes

We can add to this list all day long.

Also, know that you can always reach out to snapthegap and we will help you. Send a message, fill out the form, ask for help.

If you are stuck, the best thing to do is to ask.

You can reach snapthegap by going to the web site and under the menu item titled Stuck? you can leave your questions. You might just need a quick answer to your question — or more detail to think through and work out a more complex situation. Go ahead and ask.

We are here to help you.

Summary

Tom Hackett, university professor and former vice president of human resources says:

"SNAP exceeds my expectations. Some highlights I particularly enjoyed and value are as follows:

✓ SNAP is for leaders, managers and front line practitioners.

✓ Remember, SNAP can be used immediately, out of the box.

✓ SNAP is neither expensive nor complex.

✓ SNAP skills can and will improve with use."

That basically sums it up.

Find a workflow. Find a spot to insert a SNAP message. Do it now. SNAP is available for you immediately, out of the box. Use SNAP consistently. Listen to your customers and improve your SNAP statements. Continue to use SNAP. Develop your SNAP habit. Review and improve again, and again, and again. Don't listen to those excuses. They will come to you and will come from others. Don't listen to them. Choose to use SNAP. Be strong. Be creative. Connect with your customers. Care about outcomes and results. Become a SNAP master.

SNAP is yours; it is all about you. It will help you be more effective, more productive, less stressed and in greater control.

SNAP is your customer's; it is all about your customer. It will help them better understand what you are doing for them. It will help their perception about your service levels. It will allow your customers to be less stressed. They will experience higher levels of service.

SNAP is all about your company. If you care about your company, use SNAP to drive customer loyalty. To drive revenue.

Out SNAP your competition.

Thank you for taking time to explore SNAP. The challenge now is for you to choose to use and embrace SNAP. Put it to use. Push it. Pummel it. Pound it. Put it to the test. Become proud of your SNAP abilities.

Know that your initial use of SNAP will be simple, basic and not overly sophisticated. And that is good. Let your use of SNAP start small, nurture it. Be consistent with your use. Don't settle for that one, first statement. Use that first statement, and add more. Go ahead, add more.

Please, continue to focus on expectations. This idea is not new; it has been around for centuries.

"Life is largely a matter of expectation." This is attributed to Horace, Roman poet and historian, who lived from 65 BC to 8 BC. Yes, centuries ago, he wrote about expectations.

Know that expectations are a part of the human condition. Use SNAP to set expectations and then meet and exceed them.

The absolutely most difficult part of SNAP is that it is here, it is now. It costs you nothing. You can use it right away. You can train yourself. You don't need to be an expert before you start. You don't need permission. You don't need to do anything but go ahead and use SNAP.

So, go ahead and use SNAP.

Use it today.

Books Referenced

Business Process Outsourcing
Edward E. Lawler III, Dave Ulrich, Jac Fitz-Enz
and James C. Madden V

Crucial Confrontations
Kerry Patterson, Joseph Grenny, Ron McMillan and
Al Switzler

Customers For Life
Carl Sewell and Paul B. Brown

Execution, The Discipline of Getting Things Done
Larry Blossidy and Ram Charan

Flawless Consulting
Peter Block

From Good to Great
Jim Collins

Results That Last
Quint Studer

Smart Trust
Stephen M. R. Covey

Surf Better
Dave Rearwin

The HR Value Proposition
Dave Ulrich and Wayne Brockbank

The Power of Habit
Charles Duhigg

The Power of Less
Leo Babauta

The Toyota Way
Jeffrey Liker

Thinking for a Change
John C. Maxwell

Today Matters
John C. Maxwell

As A Man Thinketh
James Allen

A Sense of Urgency
John P. Kotter

What Really Works
William Joyce, Nitin Nohria and Bruce Roberson

When Good Isn't Good Enough
Ron Willingham

Winning
Jack Welch

Other Resources

Copies of this book are available from snapthegap.com or from Amazon.com.

Additional information and discussions are available on the snapthegap blog.

Philip is available for help as you draft out your SNAP messages. Feel free to email, or open a focused discussion on the site. More focused assistance can be arranged on a case by case basis. Please ask.

Case studies and examples will also be available on the snapthegap site.

Updates to the book will be posted and shared on the snapthegap site.

Training materials and related resources are available on the snapthegap site.

About the Author

Philip Espinosa is an experienced executive with a track record of success in improving service levels, reducing operational overhead, cost savings and spearheading large-scale projects and programs. He has a special interest in helping teams achieve success. Key roles serving in the military, the public sector and in healthcare formed his approach to service and efficiency. He believes that excellent service starts with delivering outcomes the customer values and that intentional focus is the cornerstone of effectiveness.

With a bachelor's degree in journalism and a master's degree in business, he has focused on connecting with customers in order to deliver value. He describes value as a result of partnering with people: People > Partnerships > Value.

Philip worked at The Library of Congress; with an agency providing communications support to the White House; and, with healthcare systems in Michigan, Pennsylvania and New Mexico. While serving in the U.S. Army at The Pentagon he learned the importance of keeping key customers (senior military officials) informed: the beginnings of SNAP were formed.

His belief is that success comes from listening to the customer. "There always seemed to be those customers who were satisfied," he says, "while others were not. Discounting for the occasional personality disorder, the differences seem to boil down to the expectation gap. Success for me is managing that gap, and delivering the results that my customers value."

Philip has used the SNAP technique with teams to run software projects, large scale recruiting efforts, to lead and participate with merger and acquisitions, to staff new facilities, and to support the most basic of daily, routine customer transactions.

He is a contributor to the leadership site
www.hrcsuite.com.

You can read more about SNAP at the web site:
ww.snapthegap.com

Thank You

A book is not written in isolation.

I would like to give a special thanks to my wife, Mindi, for putting up with the many — perhaps, too many — hours I spent "on the computer" with this project, for her critiques and honest input. Thank you to my parents, Dr. and Mrs. Alvaro Espinosa, for ideas and suggestions that kept me grounded.

And to many others, including: Tomas Miller; Toni R. Linn; Thomas Hackett; Scott James; Kevin Hurlahe, Tom Roberts; Monica Treacy; Martin Espinosa; Erica Miller; Roger Kohn; Katherine Espinosa, Jeremy Kuhne, Whitney Kuhne and Eddie Smith. This project would not be complete without their input, ideas and comments.

Disclaimer

Made in the USA
Columbia, SC
17 March 2023

13843237R00114